The Other Side of the Sky

A Memoir

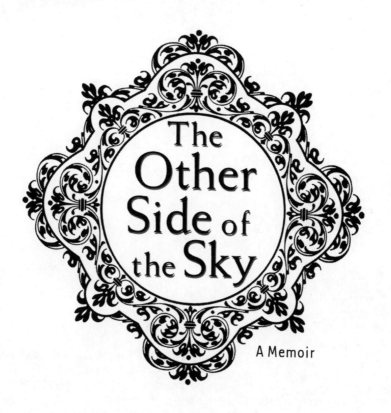

The Other Side of the Sky

A Memoir

Farah Ahmedi with Tamim Ansary

HAMPTON-BROWN

Hampton-Brown
P.O. Box 223220
Carmel, California 93922
800-333-3510
www.hampton-brown.com

Printed in the United States of America

ISBN-13: 978-0-7362-3173-2
ISBN-10: 0-7362-3173-0

10 11 12 13 14 15 10 9 8 7 6

CONTENTS

INTRODUCTION

In 2004, the television show *Good Morning, America* held a contest. The producer wanted to hear stories of everyday people overcoming **adverse** conditions. Anyone could enter by writing a summary about his or her experiences. People who watched the show could choose one story out of thousands to become a published book. The viewers chose a story by a teenager from Afghanistan named Farah Ahmedi. Soon, people all over America would know about her life in Afghanistan. They would hear about her journey to the United States. They would learn how she struggled to **integrate** into life in the United States. They would see how as a Muslim, Afghan, and now an American, Farah rebuilt her life.

Farah was born during a time of war in Afghanistan. Afghan Communists took control in 1978. After that, Farah saw different groups try to control her country. A group of Afghan rebels called the mujahideen first took power. Then the Soviet Union invaded. War in Farah's country continued between different groups for many years. Life became even harder when a strict group called the Taliban took power.

Key Concepts

adverse *adj.* difficult, harmful

integrate *v.* to fit in; to feel a part of

The Taliban made new laws. These laws took away many of the freedoms people had. Women could no longer leave home without men to protect them. They also had to wear clothes that covered everything except their eyes and hands. Men and women feared violence, even death, if they left their homes.

Because the Afghan people were tired of war, they did not fight back against the Taliban. Many tried to leave Afghanistan to find **asylum** in other countries. Like Farah, these refugees are now members of communities all over the world.

Afghanistan and Surrounding Area

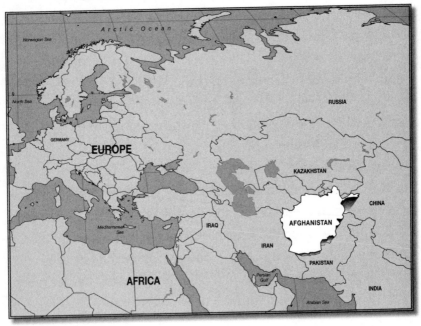

Key Concepts

asylum *n.* safety, protection

War left behind many problems in Afghanistan. One of the biggest problems was landmines. Landmines are bombs buried below the ground. They explode when something touches them. The landmines were meant to stop soldiers, but ordinary people often stepped on them and suffered terrible injuries or death. Farah was one of those injured.

In spite of her problems, Farah relied on her **faith** and her **endurance** to survive. When she left her city of Kabul in Afghanistan, an organization called World Relief helped her find a home in the United States. World Relief and organizations like it continue to help people in war-torn countries. People must go through an application and interview process to be chosen. World Relief helps them start new lives in their new countries.

Farah's journey led her to many places around the world. Now she has adjusted to life in the United States. She has learned about the kindness of strangers and about herself. Her life story shows how people can live better lives, even when their old lives are destroyed.

Key Concepts

faith *n.* beliefs, religion

endurance *n.* strength against pain and suffering

PROLOGUE

⬿⬲⬷

Alyce wanted me to share the story of my life. I told her that I wasn't ready, that it was too soon. I'm not even nineteen years old, and I haven't achieved anything yet. But Alyce said that with a life like mine, surviving itself is an achievement— just surviving.

I don't know if she's right. When I look back at my childhood in Afghanistan, it seems so far away and long ago. Back then I thought I would grow up and grow old in the city of Kabul, surrounded by my big, complicated, loving family. **Little did I know** I would lose most of them before I turned fourteen.

As a child, gazing at the high walls around our home compound, I longed to see what lay on the other side of my city. I never dreamed that I would see our home **reduced to rubble**

....

Little did I know I didn't know
reduced to rubble destroyed

and would end up living on the other side of the world, in the suburbs of a city called Chicago.

But in the end, I have decided to tell this story because it is not mine alone. It is the story of many people. Probably, you have **read the numbers**. So many people have stepped on land mines, so many have gotten hurt by war, have lost their families, fled their homes. Each of us has a story. What happened to me—both the bad and the good—really does happen to people.

I say "the bad and the good" because out of my losses have come tremendous gifts as well. Looking back, I see that my life could have ended so many times, except for unexpected strangers who reached out to me in loving kindness. After I lost my leg, I thought I could never know happiness again, and yet **that very loss opened the world to me in strange ways** and showed me wonders that I had never imagined.

I have seen my dreams crushed, but new ones have **sprouted in their place**, and some of those dreams have even come true. I have lost loved ones but not love itself. That's what my story is about, I think. That's the story I want to share with you now, the story of my life, so far.

....

read the numbers heard about how many people died

that very loss opened the world to me in strange ways the loss of my leg let me have new opportunities

sprouted in their place replaced them

THE GONDOLA

Even though ten years have passed, I still find it difficult to talk about the land mine. I don't like to think about it either, but **on that score I don't always get to choose**. One time last summer my new American friends, Alyce and John, took me to a carnival here in the suburbs of Chicago, where I live now with my mother. What a dazzling sight it was for a seventeen-year-old girl who had lived most of her life in Afghanistan and in the refugee camps of Pakistan. I had never seen anything like it—the colors, lights, noise, and **spectacle**. I ate cotton candy and **tried my luck at** a few sideshow games, and then we went to look at the rides.

We came to one called the Gondola. It was shaped like a large boat suspended from two long poles. It had many rows

....

on that score I don't always get to choose I can't control
what I think

spectacle excitement

tried my luck at played

of seats, all facing the center. The boat was swinging back and forth when we arrived. Each time it swung in one direction, the seats on that side lifted way up, maybe a hundred feet into the air. Then it swung the other way, and the seats on the other side lifted up. It was kind of like a massive swing that went from side to side instead of forward and backward.

As the ride got going faster, people started screaming, but Alyce told me they were having fun. She said the ride scared them, but they wanted to be scared. That was what they enjoyed about the ride.

I told Alyce I wanted to try it. Alyce wasn't so sure about that, but I insisted I could handle it. So she bought some tickets, and we both climbed aboard. We went to the very end of the boat, to the seats that rose the very highest, because we wanted the full effect, the biggest scare—the most fun. The man came through and locked down a bar in front of us. That bar keeps you from falling out when the ride is going. Of course, you can still get out by climbing over the bar, but when the Gondola is swinging back and forth at full speed, who would want to?

At first the ship swung slowly. It didn't go very far in either direction. But gradually, the boat went faster and swung farther. Each swing took our seats higher, and when the boat reached the top of its swing, it seemed to pause. For an instant I felt weightless. Then, when it swung the other way, I felt as if I was falling fast. **My heart came into my throat, and my throat dropped down into my stomach.** It was scary but **exhilarating**, and I was loving that feeling of speed and of the

----

My heart came into my throat, and my throat dropped down into my stomach. I felt scared and sick.

exhilarating exciting

wind in my hair.

But then at the peak of the ride, just as the boat reversed direction and our seats began to fall, the machinery sent off some kind of spark. And when that spark flashed in my eyes, it triggered something. **I dropped through a trapdoor into some other reality.** Suddenly, I wasn't in America on a carnival ride. I was on the ground, looking up into the sky and the sun. I had fallen out of that day and into a moment ten years in the past. Above me what I saw was that ring of faces, the people who **had gathered around to gawk** at me after the land mine went off—it was as real to me as the clouds overhead.

So I started screaming, right there on the Gondola ride, just like I did on that terrible day. "Why don't you help me? Why are you all just looking at me like that? Help me, someone help me!"

It was that scene, exactly. I tried to get up, as I had that day. I wanted to be **whole** again. I scrambled to get away from the horror of what had happened—except that I was not really on the ground in Afghanistan. I was at a carnival in Wheaton, Illinois, on the Gondola, struggling to get out of my seat on a ride that was going a hundred miles an hour, back and forth, up and down. Thank God Alyce was there by my side, as she has been by my side so often in these last few years. Thank God she knew at once what I was about to do, and she flung her arms around me and kept me in my place and shook me and called into my ear, "Wake up, Farah! Wake up!"

I came back to consciousness. The ride was still going, and I knew vaguely where I was, but only through the fog of a terror

....

I dropped through a trapdoor into some other reality. I felt as though I were somewhere else.

had gathered around to gawk stood near to look

whole uninjured

that I couldn't blink away. I yelled, "Stop the ride, stop the ride!"

But of course they didn't stop the ride. They never stop the ride.

I screamed, but my screams attracted no attention. Everyone was screaming. They expect people to scream on carnival rides. I was doing **nothing newsworthy**. If I had managed to get out of my seat and over the restraining bar, yes, then someone would have noticed. If I had managed to jump from the Gondola ride at the peak of its motion, yes, I would have made the news: ONE-LEGGED AFGHAN GIRL JUMPS FROM CARNIVAL RIDE. But it didn't happen because Alyce was there to save my life—but then, Alyce has done that in a lot of ways, big and small, since we met two years ago.

The ride finally slowed down, and the world around me changed from a blur of motion to a field of happy crowds enjoying a summer day. I said, "Oh my goodness, what happened?" I looked around and said, "Oh my goodness! I'm not in Afghanistan. It's not that day. I'm in America." Nothing was broken, I was told. The machine was supposed to make sparks.

Even now, I wonder what triggered my flashback at that carnival. Was it the heart-swelling sensation of falling? Was it the light that flashed in my eyes and then **morphed** into the sunlight of that awful day, the sunlight that shone through that ring of horrified faces? I wish I knew so I could get ready for the next time or avoid **tripping another switch** that turns some ordinary moment into a horrible waking dream.

Nowadays I don't dream about my leg very much. It's

....

nothing newsworthy what everyone else was doing

morphed changed

tripping another switch anything that might cause me to remember something

not like those first few weeks or even months after it was **amputated**, when I used to dream that I was riding a bicycle or running around in our yard in Kabul or just walking.

In those dreams I would say, *Oh my gosh, look at this! I can ride a bicycle. I'm running. What was I worrying about? My leg is just fine!* I don't have those kinds of dreams anymore. Now when I take off my **prosthetic** leg at night, I feel like I have always been this way. Although my mind remembers another time. They say that amputees can feel their missing limbs, but I never have. I don't feel pain, absence, presence, or any other sensation where my leg used to be. My body knows it's gone. It's just my mind that sometimes forgets. The other night I woke up thirsty and wanted a glass of water, so I automatically started to get out of bed. I almost fell, and then I remembered that I had to put on my prosthesis.

My mother and I are safe now, living in Carol Stream, Illinois. We have good food and decent shelter, and I have a dear friend. I should be contented now. I should be happy every day, every minute, every instant. It troubles me that I'm discontent and sad so much of the time.

In that last hour of school each day I'm so tired that my body hurts, and I say to myself, *As soon as I get home, I'll go to sleep, first thing.* But when I get home, I feel restless. Then I have to finish my homework. After that I eat dinner and watch TV. By ten o'clock I'm so sleepy that I hate TV, even if a good show is on. I turn it off and think, *Now, finally, I'll go to sleep.* As soon

....

amputated removed
prosthetic not real; artificial

as my head touches the pillow, however, **sleep scatters to the winds**. **The anxieties begin to churn.** If I was lonely that day, I'll feel it more intensely now. If I did poorly on a test, I'll begin to worry about it now, with the lights out and the darkness all around me.

And then some little thing that happened during the day will trigger a memory from my past. I'll get to ruminating about where I was then and where I am now. I'll start to mull over how it would be if my father were alive today, if Afghanistan had not plunged into war, if I were living in Kabul now, if I still had my whole family. Maybe I would be married or at least have **prospects**. Probably, my life would be calm. I would not have to struggle so hard each day. My mother would have grandchildren from her sons. My father would be happy, and his business would be growing.

I think of all that could have been.

And yet our life here is good. We have everything we could ask for, God be praised. I don't have to worry about money. We get **disability** from the government. I just have to go to school. I come home to a nice apartment. I see my mom and know she is feeling much better. Then Alyce calls, and we tell jokes and trade stories about our day. I feel loved.

How can I possibly feel unhappy sometimes? I have no right to sorrow. And yet at times I find I can't enjoy what I have. I come home through empty streets to our quiet little apartment, to my mother, who sits in her chair, rocking relentlessly hour after hour, lost in her thoughts, and I start to feel so lonely. I eat

....

sleep scatters to the winds I cannot sleep
The anxieties begin to churn. I begin to worry.
prospects someone I might marry
disability money because of my injury

something, and the food seems to have no flavor. I worry that I've lost the **capacity** for excitement that I used to have in such abundance as a little girl, living in Afghanistan with my family.

I remember the mealtimes of my childhood—I don't mean the great festival days, just the ordinary, everyday meals. My parents served all five of us children off of a single platter. When they said, "Dinner is ready," we **rushed the tablecloth**, hands unwashed. They sent us back. "Wash your hands, children!" And then we'd all be scrambling and jostling around the water pot, splashing one another and giggling. I remember the excitement of dinnertime. Five of us siblings clustered around one platter, banging elbows, chattering and gobbling. My father would tell us sternly, "It's time to eat, not talk!" And then if we were hungry, we'd worry that the others would eat up all the food before we got our portion, because we were sharing from a single platter. So we'd all settle down to **win the competition**, each of us cramming the food **away by the fistful** as fast as we could. Crowding and gobbling—it was so much fun to be one of five children eating together from a single platter. How we laughed! The taste of the food that I ate eleven or twelve years ago remains in my mouth more vividly than the food I eat today, because that's actually the memory of a kind of fun I can never have again: I'm remembering the flavor of being with my family, part of one big, loving group. We aren't that big group anymore. It's down to just the two of us now—my mother and me.

That's probably why I have so much trouble falling asleep at

....

capacity ability
rushed the tablecloth ran to eat from the same plate
win the competition eat as much as we could
away by the fistful in large amounts

night. I turn out the lights, and my head fills with thoughts that begin to circle madly through my mind. Then I imagine a big eraser inside me where my thoughts are. I rub that eraser across the **bustle and buzz**, rubbing out one memory after another, until only silence remains. Only then can I sink into the luxury of sleep.

But sleep never lasts. Sooner or later a nightmare always wakes me. In the middle of the night I can't find my eraser. My heart is pounding in my chest. I have to find another strategy for calming down. If I was dreaming about my mother dying, I listen for her breath. The sound of her coughing calms me down. Or I hear her pacing restlessly in our small apartment in the dark, as she used to do so often in our early days in America, and even that sound reassures me. I think, *She is still alive.* And then I can go back to sleep.

I have nightmares every night. I can't get away from them.

Sometimes I dream that we've gone back to Pakistan for a visit and I have lost my passport. I'm searching desperately through our baggage, strewing our clothes about, crying out loud, *What am I doing here? Why did I come back?*

Or I dream that we're in Pakistan and staying too long. Our tickets have been stamped for a certain flight. **They'll expire** if we don't get to the airport in time. But everyone keeps trying to **delay us**. My mother doesn't understand **my sense of urgency**. I'm crying out, *Let's go, let's go, before something happens, before they shut the doors!* But she's saying, *Wait, I can't find my scarf. Wait, we have to say good-bye to your aunt. Wait, we*

....

bustle and buzz terrible, violent memories
They'll expire We will not be able to use them
delay us stop us from leaving
my sense of urgency why I want to leave now

can't leave without visiting your grandparents. . . .

Sometimes I dream that Alyce won't talk to me. I've made her angry. I plead with her. I say, *This isn't right, why are you angry with me? I didn't do anything wrong, don't be mad!*

Or I see that Alyce has made a new friend. She's striking up a conversation with my cousin. I **fly into a rage** at that cousin. Why is she talking to my Alyce? *Get away from her, she's my friend!* And in real life my poor cousin isn't even in America. She's stuck back there in **dire straits**, and yet in my dreams I curse her.

Sometimes I dream that a stranger is hitting me. I want to hit back, but I can't. And then suddenly I find my mother waking me up. She tells me I was sitting up in bed, making slapping and punching motions with my arms. Oh, we laugh about it! She **paints such a comical image of** me, punching away at nothing and growling, "I'm going to slap you so hard!"

I dream that I have fallen into a river. A woman up on the riverbank is dangling a handkerchief down to me. I try to grab it, but it's too short. I try to grab it, but it's too flimsy—it tears in my grasp. I try to grab it, and I get it in my clutches; I start climbing up it, hand over hand, but the handkerchief keeps stretching out. No matter how hard I climb, my feet never leave the water. In fact, I sink deeper with that tattered handkerchief still in my grip. I feel the water in my mouth . . . in my nose. . . .

Every time my mother gets sick during the day, I dream that night that she is dying. I scream, *Take her to the hospital! Someone help us!* People have gathered around to watch us. Their eyes

....

fly into a rage am angry
dire straits a bad situation
paints such a comical image of tells such a funny story about

bulge out strangely. They find us interesting. Their eyes bulge because we fascinate them, but none of them reaches out. They seem to think we are figures in a glass case or a movie. They don't seem to realize we are right there, close enough to touch. They could take our hands. I shout at them, *We exist!*

Then I realize no one is going to help us. **It's all up to me.** I lift my mother in my arms. I will have to carry her to the hospital by myself. But as I struggle through the door, she begins to grow. My mother gets bigger and heavier in my arms. I can't carry her! I don't have the strength! She gets longer. Her feet drag on the ground, her head drags, I can't hold up her middle. I'm just too small and getting smaller. I wake up screaming.

Some of my dreams are so vivid, so full of color, so real that I can't believe I'm dreaming. When I wake up, my eyes are wet with tears. My heart is **banging against my ribs.** I tell myself, *It was only a dream, Farah, only* a dream . . . And it might or might not comfort me. It depends, because I do dream about dead people so much. I stroll with them. I talk with them. I hold them in my arms. They are all alive inside me, still. My father and grandmother appear to me, and they are reaching out and **beckoning to me, murmuring** softly, *Come, Farah. Come be with us now!* During the dream these images do not frighten me. I love my father, and I'm so glad to see him. His voice comforts me. But when I wake up in the morning, I remember what people say about the dead beckoning to you in your dreams: that it means you are going to die soon yourself.

....

It's all up to me. I am the only one who can help her.
banging against my ribs beating fast
beckoning to me, murmuring calling me, speaking

That's when I tremble.

But **it's all in my head**. That's what I have to keep telling myself. I'm safe in America now . . . and besides, they're not all terrible, the dreams I have. Lately, I dream that I've grown wings sometimes. I have feathers. I can fly. I love those dreams! I'm soaring overhead, and people are all pointing to me and exclaiming, *Look! It's Farah! She can fly! Farah can fly!*

I wake up **with a glad heart** then and feel that I *am* flying in some sense: flying into my future—and yet—the past won't let me go. Not completely. Not yet.

....

it's all in my head it isn't real

with a glad heart happy

BEFORE YOU MOVE ON...

1. **Author's Point of View** Reread pages 13–14. Why did Farah struggle with the decision to tell her story?

2. **Comparisons** Reread pages 20–21. How is Farah's life in America different from her old life in Afghanistan?

LOOK AHEAD Read to page 40 to find out how Farah's parents met.

WHERE WE CAME FROM

—⁓—

My family **roots go back to** the village near the city
of Ghazni, some ninety-two miles southwest of Kabul. A
thousand years ago Ghazni was the capital of an empire that
stretched from the Indus River to the Caspian Sea. It was a city
brimming with artists and poets and scholars. It had paved
streets and magnificent buildings—**mosques** and palaces and
towers, **covered with mosaic tiles** in shimmering designs that
looked like lace.

Today Ghazni is a small walled city of about forty thousand.
The ruins of two tall towers and a few fragments of ancient
walls are all that remain of Ghazni's glorious past. On those
towers you can still see some of the tile work, but today's
Ghazni is mainly a market town that serves as a gateway to

....

roots go back to is from
brimming filled
mosques Muslim places of worship
covered with mosaic tiles with colorful tiles all over

Hazarajat, the valley in central Afghanistan where the Hazara people—my people—mostly live.

Like most rural Afghans, the people of our village made their living as farmers. They raised animals, too—cows, buffalo, goats, sheep, and chickens. We lived in **fortresslike compounds** called *qalas*, scattered up and down the valley. My father's father was a mullah, a learned man who read the **Koran** and knew the commandments of our faith. A mullah takes care of the mosque and leads prayers on Fridays and religious holidays. He teaches youngsters to read and write and administers the rituals that mark the important stages of ordinary life.

When a baby was born, for example, my grandfather was called in to whisper the ceremonial words into the infant's ear, words that invited the child into our Islamic faith. At weddings it was my grandfather who performed the **matrimonial** ceremony. And each morning, just before dawn, it was my grandfather who climbed up into the tower of the mosque and sounded the *aazan*, the call to prayer.

My grandfather achieved his respected position when he was still a young man. As I mentioned, his duties included teaching children, teenagers, and even some adults (if they wanted) to read and write. He taught both girls and boys, but he taught them separately.

As a young man, my grandfather was engaged to be married to his cousin. A mullah is allowed to marry, just like any other man. He also may own land, grow crops, conduct business, and

----

fortresslike compounds groups of buildings surrounded by walls

Koran Muslim holy book

matrimonial marriage

do anything else that ordinary people do. There is nothing special about him except for his learning. My grandfather's parents had **arranged the match** with his cousin long before either party was **of age**. This was very common in Afghanistan, for most marriages are arranged by families there.

One girl who studied with my grandfather wore a particularly large and tightly wrapped head scarf. A proper, modest Muslim woman is supposed to keep her hair covered, but this girl's scarf covered more than her hair. It covered her whole forehead right down over her eyebrows, which is not considered necessary. My grandfather somehow got it into his head that this girl wore such a head scarf because she was bald. He began to think about this possibility day and night: Was she bald or wasn't she? It became his obsession. One day he finally couldn't take it any longer. He had to know.

That day, when the girl got up from her lesson to leave the room, the end of her long head scarf was trailing on the ground. My grandfather (accidentally-on-purpose) stepped on that bit of scarf. As the girl stood up, therefore, the scarf was pulled off her head, and my grandfather saw that not only did she have a full head of hair, but she was beautiful. He fell in love with her **on the spot**.

He went to his parents and said, "Forget about that match with my cousin. I want to marry someone else." And he told them about his beautiful student.

Well, of course this was a **scandal** in the village. What was the world coming to when a boy told his parents whom he was

....

arranged the match planned the marriage
of age old enough to marry
on the spot that moment; immediately
scandal very bad thing to do

28

going to marry instead of his parents telling him? Eventually, the arguments died down, however, and my grandfather won his parents over. The ancient engagement was broken off, and the elders did the necessary negotiating with the parents of my grandfather's beautiful student. This is how my grandparents on my father's side got together.

They had a big family, three girls and four boys. My grandfather owned some land, but he could not farm it properly because his duties as a mullah kept him too busy. As a result, in spite of all the respect he gained for his religious position, **his material circumstances declined**. He was forced to borrow large sums of money on several occasions.

In Islam it is **illegal to charge interest** for a loan. So, when people borrow money, they give the lender some form of valuable moneymaking collateral. The lender holds that property and makes use of it as if it were his own until he gets his money back. Essentially, you might say that in order to borrow money, you have to **pawn** something of value. My grandfather was forced to pawn his lands. Without land, he had no way to make money, so he could not get his lands out of hock. For all intents and purposes, once he borrowed money, my grandfather became a landless peasant.

His son Ghulam Hussein—my father—decided to do something about this. When my father came of age, he went to Kabul. I say "came of age," but he was actually still a teenager. In Kabul he apprenticed himself to a master tailor, learned the trade, and worked hard. In fact, he barely stopped to eat or

....

his material circumstances declined he had less money and property

illegal to charge interest against the law to make people pay extra money

pawn sell

sleep. One time, so the family story goes, when he stood up, one of his trouser legs fell right off: It had worn away at the knees because my father had been sitting on the ground for so many hours and days on end, cutting and sewing.

The hard work paid off, however. After several years my father was able to return to our village with cash in his pocket. He paid off his father's debts, got the family lands back, and restored my family to landowner status. This **feat made quite a loud noise** in our valley: a son saving his father from **penury**. And he was scarcely more than a boy! The news spread to other villages, and people came to regard my father as a sort of hero. **His name began to sound from many lips.**

Well, once my father had squared away the family fortunes, he returned to Kabul and went back to work. He graduated out of apprentice status and became a tailor in his own right, but he went on working just as hard or harder than before.

When he next returned to the village and turned his savings over to his parents, his mother kissed him on the head and said, "What a good son you are! You have certainly earned a reward. This time we will find you a wife."

So my grandmother began to ask around. She asked all the women in her village if they knew of a girl worthy to marry the famous hero Ghulam Hussein. One of her neighbors said yes, she did indeed know of just such a girl for my father. She was the daughter of the *malik*, or chieftain, of a village a few miles up the valley.

A *malik's* daughter sounded good to my grandmother. She

....

feat made quite a loud noise accomplishment made him famous

penury being without money; poverty

His name began to sound from many lips. People began to talk about him.

said, "Take me there."

Well, her neighbor was on visiting terms with the *malik's* family, so she took my grandmother there for an overnight visit. Their arrival caused a **great hubbub** in the *malik's* household. "The mother of Ghulam Hussein has come to see us," people said. "The mother of that famous hero has come. What can she want?"

During the visit my grandmother looked about at all the girls of the household and spotted the one her neighbor must have meant, a beautiful girl but a shy one. This girl kept her distance. In fact, she stayed out of sight in the back rooms as much as she could, having assumed that the visitors had come to discuss some sort of **solemn** business, possibly related to land. She never thought their visit had anything to do with her. That's my mother's **modesty**.

But when she came into the room to serve some food to the guests, my grandmother said to her, "Fatima-jan! Come over here and help me out. I seem to have a splinter in my finger." She said this just to draw the girl close so she could get a good look at her and see if she was really as beautiful as she seemed from a distance. My mother came over and dutifully began to look for the splinter in her future mother-in-law's finger. Suddenly, she felt the intensity of my grandmother's gaze. Looking up, she realized in a flash that this woman had come looking for a bride. Embarrassment and panic swept over her, and she ran away—but my grandmother had seen all that she needed to see. This girl **would do**.

....

great hubbub lot of excitement
solemn serious
modesty humble way
would do was good enough for her son

Returning home, she discussed the matter with her husband and her son and soon went back to the *malik* with a **delegation** from her *qala* to formally **seek Fatima's hand for her son**. My mother's parents didn't play hard to get, as is common in such wedding negotiations. They didn't say, *Oh, we can't, she's too young, this is so unexpected, come back another day, we have to get over the tizzy you have put us in.* They were all too happy to say yes to a match between their daughter and the famous hero Ghulam Hussein, the boy who had saved his father's land. Besides, the son of a mullah marrying the daughter of a *malik*— this looked like a fitting match to both families and to all the relatives on either side. The agreement was quickly made, therefore, and my parents got engaged.

At the *shirnee-khuree*, the "candy-eating"—the party that celebrates an engagement—my parents saw each other for the first time. My father was sitting near my mother, gazing upon her, gladdened by what he saw. My mother was too shy to look up. She kept her gaze fixed modestly on the floor in front of her. But inside, of course, she was dying of curiosity. Finally, she did turn her head stealthily to steal just a peep, if she could, of her husband-to-be. Unfortunately, my father was sitting a little too far back for her to see him. A lamp behind him cast his shadow on the floor. Because the light was so close to him, his shadow looked huge. That shadow was my mother's first impression of my father. She thought her parents had **betrothed her to** an enormous fat man, and she panicked. Later, when she found that he was of normal size and such a

....

delegation large group

seek Fatima's hand for her son ask if Fatima could marry her son

betrothed her to let her marry

pleasant fellow, and so good-looking to boot, she was relieved and delighted.

My parents were engaged for two years. When they finally got married, the wedding lasted seven days. Of course, that wasn't unusual for a village wedding, but my grandmother said they staged a truly extraordinary wedding for my parents, a wedding that **resounded in the folklore** of the village for years to come. For example, instead of using kerosene lanterns at that party, they used expensive hurricane lamps, which shed a brilliant and steady light. (The village had no electricity at the time.)

Eight men carried my mother several miles from her village to ours in a portable covered throne with handles extending in front and in back for men to bear on their shoulders. A great festive crowd surrounded and accompanied the **procession**, singing and beating drums. When they arrived at the groom's village, they took my mother into the wedding chamber, and there the women swarmed around and fussed over her. They fixed her hair and put the beauty dots on her cheeks, and then they wrapped her in a big scarf, because she certainly wasn't going to show her face to just anyone. Not only did she wear that scarf over her head, but she kept a big white handkerchief in front of her face throughout the wedding. Technically, my father was supposed to see her for the first time at the wedding, but actually, they had gotten to know each other quite well during their two-year engagement period. Still, they **went through the ritual** in which a blanket is thrown over the couple

....

resounded in the folklore was talked about again and again in the stories

procession wedding group

went through the ritual experienced the ceremony

so they can look at each other's faces in a mirror, supposedly for the first time. This is how things were done in an Afghan village just thirty or forty years ago, when my parents got married; it's how things are still done in much of Afghanistan today.

Well, my parents started living together, but over that next year quarrels broke out between my father and the head of his village. Everywhere else in the valley, people were still talking about my father's achievements in Kabul and marveling over the money he had made and how he had gotten his own father out of debt. The head of our village got jealous of our family. He said my father was **putting on airs** and behaving as if he thought he was better than other people.

Finally, my father couldn't stand it anymore. He said to his parents, "Come on, let's move to the city." So in 1976 my father and his parents and siblings all moved to Kabul. They rented a small compound in the southwestern section of the city, and my father began supporting the family as a tailor.

Afghanistan was going through great changes at the time. Kabul was becoming a modern city. My mother used to tell me how it was in the capital when she first moved there, and later, too, when the Russians occupied the city. In those days, she said, city women went to work outside the home. They wore stockings instead of the traditional **baggy pantaloons**. They didn't wear veils or even head scarves. They appeared on TV, where they read the news, sang songs, and even performed dances.

All these changes were **spurring** arguments and tensions

....

putting on airs bragging
baggy pantaloons loose pants
spurring causing

between city folks and country folks. In villages like the one my parents came from, people said the city folks had abandoned our Afghan customs, our traditions, and our religion. They said the city people were becoming **corrupt**. Even in the city, people had different attitudes about the changes. I guess some people can handle drastic change and embrace it, and others can't. Some people want change; some don't.

In those days my father made a Western-style outfit for my mother. He told her, "Don't wear a head scarf anymore. Cut your hair, be modern." But my mother was a traditional woman, and on this point she refused to go along with her husband's wishes. "I won't do it," she said. "I don't want to be a 'modern' woman."

Meanwhile, politics were **heating up** in our country. Three years before my parents moved to Kabul, the last king of Afghanistan had been **overthrown** by his own cousin, Sardar Daoud, who quickly began ruling the country as a military **dictator**. Daoud called himself a "president," but he was a member of the same royal dynasty that had ruled Afghanistan for almost two hundred years.

Two years after my parents moved to Kabul, an Afghan Communist party overthrew that so-called president and ended the dynasty. These Afghan Communists had nothing to do with royalty or Afghan aristocracy. For the first time in my country's history a political party, rather than a family, held power, and the leaders of this party were people without prestigious connections or famous family names.

....

corrupt dishonest
heating up becoming violent
overthrown defeated
dictator leader that rules alone

At first these changes at the top did not affect our family much. My family members had nothing to do with politics, as they were actually practiced, and none of them held any government positions. Violence **broke out sporadically** in the city among competing factions of Communists, but when gun battles or political murders took place in some other neighborhood, my parents usually did not even hear about it until later, and then just as stories. Ordinary people did not really feel threatened in everyday life, especially not in their own neighborhoods.

My father was gaining a reputation as a tailor, and his business was growing—this was the big news for the family. My father was making good money, and my mother was working side by side with him, managing that money. Each week my father gave her a certain amount of cash to cover family expenses, and she **allocated the money to** various uses, hunting up the best bargains and tracking every coin spent. She was so good at money management that she saved about half of what he gave her each week.

Eventually, she used those savings to buy a gold necklace and other gold jewelry. This was not **ostentation**. In Afghanistan traditional women don't keep their money in a bank; they **keep it on their own persons**, in the form of jewelry. You might say that women wear their life savings. My mother told everyone that her husband had bought all that gold for her. She didn't mention the part she played with her money-management skills. In short, she gave all the credit to my father,

....

broke out sporadically happened sometimes
allocated the money to saved the money for
ostentation to impress others
keep it on their own persons wear it

in order to elevate his reputation. He appreciated what she did for him. My parents had a good marriage.

Then, at the end of 1979, the Soviets invaded Afghanistan. At first even this made no real difference to ordinary people like my father. He **went on plying his trade**. The Soviet troops secured Kabul against looters and thugs, murderers and **rebels**. On an everyday level, in what was soon to be my neighborhood, life went on more or less peacefully. My brother told me that during the Soviet occupation of Afghanistan, they would often see Russian soldiers on the street and would boldly ask them for candy. They were not particularly afraid of the Russians.

Very soon, however, the Soviets did start to make war on the rest of the country. Their planes took off from air bases near Kabul and bombed various villages. They were out to defeat rebels called mujahideen, who were rallying the rural people against Soviet rule. These rebels were emerging all over the country, in all the villages. When the government dropped bombs to get rid of the rebels, it also drove many villagers from their homes. Hundreds of thousands of families streamed south or west, trying to get out of the country, hoping to find safety in Pakistan or Iran.

For most Afghans, however, the nearest border lay far away, across a dangerous landscape, a journey of many days, and those who fled the country **forfeited** everything they owned. Leaving the country was therefore a big decision that not everyone was willing to embrace. Millions fled, but millions more stayed.

....

went on plying his trade continued working as a tailor
rebels people who fought against Soviet power
forfeited gave up

Many of the **latter** still had to leave their bombed-out villages, though. They made their way to the nearest place where bombs were not falling. And the single safest place from **Soviet bombardment** was Kabul, because that is where the Soviets themselves lived. In just a few years, therefore, that pleasant city filled up with refugees from the villages and **swelled into a bloated metropolis full of sprawling slums**.

Yet, while all these momentous events were going on in the country at large, my family remained absorbed in its own private dramas. Our relatives were moving to the city in bunches, and each time a new family arrived, they came right to my father; because he was doing well and had sunk some roots in the city, they assumed he could find them jobs and places to live.

He did what he could, but there was only so much he could do. My father was supporting his siblings as well as his parents. He paid for his brothers' weddings, which is no small thing, because in Afghanistan the groom is responsible for all wedding costs and he must pay **a dowry** as well. The cost of marriage keeps many poor men single their whole lives. Thanks to my father, however, my uncles escaped this fate. With my grandmother's help, my father also found husbands for his sisters.

The family compound in southwest Kabul was not a tiny place, but it could not compare to those fortress-compounds in the villages. With my married uncles living there, along with sporadic newcomers from the village, it grew too crowded.

At last my father told his brothers, "Look, fellows, you're all

---

latter people who stayed

Soviet bombardment being hit by Soviet bombs

swelled into a bloated metropolis full of sprawling slums became a big city full of poor people

a dowry with expensive gifts

grown up now. If you want to work with me, that's fine. I'll take you on as apprentices, and I'll pay you wages, as I would any other apprentice. But you must move out and start your own households. The time has come, and that's the way it has to be."

All the old quarrels **flared up** again, the old charges of arrogance and pride and grandiosity. My uncles accused my father of treating his own family as if they were strangers. It was all part of the conflict between an old way of life and a new way of life. My father leaned toward modern ways. He wanted to be part of a new, socially modern Afghanistan, and this included the idea of **nuclear families** living in separate households. He and his brothers **fell out over** these issues. Finally, his brothers moved out in a huff. The truth is, their wives were pressing them as well. Quite understandably, my uncles' wives wanted households of their own.

In any case, **fault lines sprang up** within my larger clan, endless small feuds that got patched up on holidays and flared up again soon after. Once they left, my uncles never did work with my father again. They tried different trades. One went into the army. Another tried to open his own tailor shop. When that failed, he worked as a plasterer. My uncles never quite found their footing. They never caught up with my ever-more-successful father, and as a result, they could never quite forgive him for quarrels they had forgotten the sources of.

Meanwhile, my mother had her own torment. Four years after getting married, she had still not gotten pregnant. She consulted doctors. The doctors said there was nothing wrong

....

flared up started
nuclear families the parents and children
fell out over argued about
fault lines sprang up arguments happened

with her, and they could therefore do nothing to help her. She consulted mullahs; they told her to pray. She prayed and wept and prayed some more. She visited the shrines of saints and bought **amulets**. Nothing worked. During the course of all this my mother developed a little cough—the first sign of a problem that would virtually cripple her in later life. Our relatives were beginning to mutter. "The woman is sickly and **barren**," they whispered to my father. "You should start looking for a second wife, someone who can give you children." Chatter of this sort wounded my mother deeply.

And then, at last, it happened: Just after the Soviet army poured into Kabul, my mother got pregnant. A moment of tremendous terror for the country coincided with a moment of tremendous celebration and relief in my mother's life and in the life of her little family.

That next year, as the Soviets were beginning to destroy the villages of Afghanistan, my brother Mahmoud was born. Not only had my mother given birth, but she had produced a boy. **In terms of Afghan society, her triumph was complete.** The relatives had nothing more to say. A couple of years later she gave birth to my older sister, Niloufar; and then, in 1987, at the height of the war between the mujahideen and the Soviets, I was born.

....

amulets good luck charms

barren cannot have children

In terms of Afghan society, her triumph was complete. It was very important in Afghan society to give birth to a boy.

BEFORE YOU MOVE ON...

1. **Summarize** Farah's mother and father met through her grandparents. Describe how this happened.

2. **Sequence** Reread pages 37–38. The Soviets invaded Afghanistan in 1979. What happened next?

LOOK AHEAD Read to page 57 to find out about Farah's early years in Kabul.

When I Was
Very Little

~~~

As a child, I lived a fairly happy life. What did I know about the war in the countryside? What did I know about the gun battles between various Communist factions in other parts of the city far from ours? Nothing. We heard occasional explosions, but those rockets never landed in or near our house. We heard distant gunfire, but we grew up with that sound. To us, it was just one of the noises of the city, along with traffic and the buzz of voices from the **bazaar** down the block. Sometimes we saw planes **streaking overhead**, but no one told us children where they were going or what they were doing. To us, they were just something to clap at in delight when their white smoke made dazzling patterns against the blue sky.

I didn't live in Kabul, really: I lived in our compound,

....

bazaar market
streaking overhead flying over the city

nested in my family. I knew only that this was my mother, this was my father, these were my siblings. There were five of us now. In addition to my older brother and sister, Mahmoud and Niloufar, I had a younger brother Ghayous and a baby sister Roya. I knew when I was hungry and what food I liked, and where the **corridors** led to in our house, and what I might find in the distant corners of our yard—that was my world.

It's true that even as a young child, I did sometimes leave the compound on my own. In Kabul each family makes it own dough and then takes it to a *naan-bayee*, a bread bakery, to have it baked for a small fee. Sometimes the chore of taking the family dough to the bakery **fell to me**; but the *naan-bayee* was **only a stone's throw from** our compound door.

I also went to some of my relatives' houses, if they lived in our neighborhood or nearby. The farthest I went alone was to my maternal aunt's house. She lived about a half hour's walk from us, through a maze of alleyways. She had several children and sometimes wanted me to come over and watch the youngest one, the baby. I was only five or six at the time myself, but my aunt merely needed me to let her know when the baby started crying. That much I could handle. The first three or four times I "babysat" for her, she walked me from our house to hers. After that I knew the way, and the adults let me go on my own.

But I never left the compound on my own just to explore. My mother didn't want me to play out in the alley. My older brother went out there all the time, to shoot marbles with his friends or to fly kites or just to hang around gossiping with

....

nested in safely with
corridors hallways
fell to me was mine
only a stone's throw from very close to

other neighborhood boys, but he was a boy, and he was older. If I tried to go out into the alley, my brother yelled at me. He saw himself as my guardian and the one in charge of enforcing my mother's rules. In fact, as the oldest sibling, and a boy, he felt himself to be in charge of all the rest of us. Among us kids, Mahmoud was the boss—which is the typical role of the eldest son in an Afghan family.

As a child, then, I never learned very much about Kabul. Even now, I know merely the names of a few neighborhoods. I have no sense of where they are or how the city is **laid out**. I went out a few times with my parents and saw bits of the city through a taxicab window. I went past the Mosque of the Two-Sworded King once, but I never went inside it. I saw Brick Bridge, one of Kabul's oldest bridges. I remember a trembling suspension bridge that spanned the Kabul River. My mother and I had to cross it a few times for some reason, and every time we did, I gripped her hand and clung to her skirts on the way across because the trembling of that bridge frightened me.

I did go to my father's shop sometimes, I and my siblings. My father was no longer just taking **individual commissions**. He had a business now. He bought enormous loads of **secondhand** clothes imported from Germany and modified them into garments that Afghans wanted and would buy. He opened those bags at home. Each bag bore a label that said something like 100 OVERCOATS, but you never knew what was actually inside one of those bags until you opened it. You could not **get a sneak peek**. You had to buy the bag contents unseen

....

laid out planned, arranged
individual commissions small orders for clothing
secondhand used
get a sneak peek look before you bought it

43

and **take your chances**. You might find you had bought fifty raggedy things barely recognizable as coats, forty that needed repair, and ten that someone could actually wear without **alteration**.

When my father opened a new shipment, we kids would swarm all over it, rolling in the mountains of fabric and searching the pockets for items of interest. And we always found stuff: handkerchiefs, coins, all sorts of odd little treasures. Once in a while we found a bill—it was German money and therefore no good to us; but **these little tokens from another world** intrigued us and filled us with a sense of romance and adventure.

Once we had opened a package and spread the contents around, my father would put us children to work. He gave us scissors or a razor blade and assigned each of us some number of overcoats to take apart. The younger kids might get just one or two coats, the older ones four or five. We used our razors or scissors to cut the seams and remove the buttons, hooks, zippers, labels, and other accessories. Once the younger kids had finished dismantling their assigned overcoats, they could run off and play. My father sorted the parts into piles—usable pieces of cloth here, worn-out unusable pieces there, zippers in another pile, and so on. Then he, my mother, or some of the older kids ironed the usable parts.

We didn't have an electric iron, because we did not have electricity all the time. In fact, in my neighborhood we never had electricity during the day. We had it only at night, and

---

take your chances risk buying something worthless

alteration changes

these little tokens from another world this money from a faraway place

even at night, different sides of the street took turns. One night one side of the street would light up, the next night the other side. That's how it went. So we set a flat cast-iron pot lid over a wood-burning stove and set the iron on that lid. As soon as the iron was hot, we would take it off and iron until the metal got cool, then set it on the pot lid again.

We burned the unusable scraps of leftover cloth in that stove because we didn't want to waste anything, not knowing that those rags were often made of **synthetic materials** and that the smoke from the burning plastic **was aggravating my mother's asthma**.

After all the parts had been ironed, my father cut them into new shapes and reconfigured them to make jumpers and jackets and other garments. He marketed these in a number of stores around town. Afghans liked jackets made of that heavy German overcoat cloth. Kabul winters can be bitter.

I guess I was a naughty girl, or at least, when I think back to my childhood, I remember getting into mischief. Once, for example, when I was taking our dough to the bakery, I spilled the tray. The balls of dough fell on the ground. They got covered with dust and twigs. I just put them back on the tray and went on to the *naan-bayee*. When I brought the bread back, people ate it without comment, even though I could detect sand and gravel and bark and bits of wood in it.

Another time my brother bought a bunch of baby chickens. A few shops in our local bazaar had gotten **incubator** machines. They would put eggs into the machines and hatch hundreds of

....

synthetic materials man-made, artificial fabric

was aggravating my mother's asthma made my mother have more difficulty breathing

incubator egg heating

chicks at a time. People bought the baby chicks because they were cute. It was a **fad that swept** Kabul.

In any case, my brother bought a dozen chicks one day. The next morning he had to go to school, so he told me to take care of them. I promised him I would. He kept his chicks in a big cardboard box, and as soon as he left, I decided to have a look. I wanted to see how the cute little things were doing. I saw that they had knocked over their water bowl and were getting their tiny feet all wet. I thought that their bowl was way too small, that they needed a bowl they couldn't knock over. So I filled a large, heavy, pewter pan with water and set it in the carton for the chicks.

Then I went off to play and forgot all about them.

When my brother came home, he looked in the carton and saw all his chicks floating upside down in the pewter pan. They had climbed into it, and then they couldn't get out and they drowned. He was so mad at me, he dumped that pan of water right over my head!

On another occasion my brother asked me to warm up some milk for him. I did this, but then I set the cup on a table while I went to get some sugar. When I came back, a **feral** cat had gotten into the house, and it was busy enjoying my brother's milk. No one keeps cats as pets in Afghanistan, but every house has dozens of feral ones hanging around, looking for scraps. I chased this one away. The glass was still fairly full. The cat hadn't **lapped up** much. I got to thinking: If I told my brother about the cat, he would **scold** me and probably refuse to drink the milk. If I poured the milk out and got him a fresh cup, my mother might yell at me for wasting precious milk. So I just stirred the sugar into the milk and gave it to him without mentioning the cat. He never knew. To this day, I feel a little guilty about it.

One time I stole a cookie. In Afghanistan people make a kind of cookie called rote for festive occasions. That year my mother made rote for Eid, the holiest Muslim holiday. The rote was just for guests, and I knew it, but I sneaked in and stole one cookie out of the box. When I tried to eat it, though, I felt too nervous to **get it down**. I managed to nibble just a few bites out of it and that was all. But I couldn't put the nibbled cookie back in the box now—everyone would know! On the other hand, I could not bring myself to throw away a perfectly good cookie. I didn't know what to do. So I hid it in the bedding, between two mattresses, and there it stayed for over a year. My mother found it after I had been airlifted to Germany. The cookie left a grease spot on the bedding. I am told that the moment my mother saw that cookie, she started crying. She knew I had stolen the cookie. She should have been angry at me, but instead, **her tender heart went out to** her daughter, who had missed the enjoyment of her theft.

I vividly remember another **petty theft** I committed as a child. My brother and I had gone to the bazaar to buy some yogurt cheese known as *chaka*. The vendor was charging ten afghanis for it. We put the money on his scales, and he saw us put it there. But when he went to get the *chaka*, something came

----

get it down eat it all
her tender heart went out to she was so kind she felt sad
thinking about
petty theft minor crime

over me, and I snatched the money back and put it in my pocket.

When he returned with the *chaka*, he said, "Did you pay me?"

My brother said, "Yes. We put the money right there on the scales. Don't you remember?"

"Oh, yes," said the shopkeeper. "I must have put it away in my drawer."

So I **got away with stealing**. A few nights later we kids were huddled under blankets, keeping warm, and my mother was telling us stories. She told us one story about a little boy who stole an egg. His mother knew about it, but she didn't say anything to him. So the next day he stole a chicken. The mother still didn't say anything. She just cooked up the chicken for the family dinner. After that the boy went on stealing and **so slipped into a life of crime**. Finally, one day he **committed some truly heinous deed** and was caught. He was hauled before the judge and sentenced to be hanged. After they put the noose around his neck, they said, "Do you have any last request?"

"Yes," he said, "I want to see my mother."

They sent someone to fetch his mother. She came up to him, weeping and wailing. He said to her, "Mother, stick out your tongue." Puzzled though she was, she did as her son asked. He grabbed her tongue and cut it off. He said, "You share the blame for my crimes. If you had punished me when I was young, I would not be standing here wearing a noose today."

---

got away with stealing stole without getting in trouble

so slipped into a life of crime started doing crimes that were worse

committed some truly heinous deed did something really bad

After hearing that story, I felt sick with worry and made myself a private promise never to lie or cheat or steal again. Meanwhile, **in the larger world**, in the war-torn country all around me, people were being slaughtered for no crime at all, many of them children just like me. Maybe at that very moment someone was planting the land mine that would **soon plunge my small life into horror**.

---

in the larger world in the rest of Afghanistan
soon plunge my small life into horror make my life horrible

Going to School

─◦◦◦─

When I was six, something wonderful happened. I started school. My mother took me there every day for the first week to show me the way. It was a ten- or fifteen-minute walk from our house—down to the end of our alley, then past some open fields, and then along a larger road.

I don't remember what the place was called. **I'm not good with** names. But I remember that it had a large courtyard surrounded by a ring of classrooms built along the high mud walls that enclosed **the entire complex**.

Here in America, first and second graders study in brightly painted rooms filled with books and art supplies and featuring all sorts of posters and pictures on the walls. In Afghanistan our classrooms were **naked chambers** with nothing on the walls

....

I'm not good with I cannot remember
the entire complex the whole group of buildings
naked chambers empty rooms

except a chalkboard.

My class had about thirty kids, half of them boys and half of them girls. The boys all sat on one side of the room, the girls on the other. We sat on benches arranged in rows, four of us to a bench. The school did not have enough benches for all the students, so we **jostled** and struggled for places every day. Those who failed to get a seat on a bench had to sit on the floor.

Getting a bench was so important that some of us children came to school early and grabbed benches from other classrooms. But the next day students from those other classrooms would come early and take their benches back. And on the next day after that students from both classrooms might come early and fight over benches. Every morning before school started, you got this scuffling and struggling over benches. It was all in good fun, though. No one got hurt. We were playing.

School was **casual** in Afghanistan, not like in America, where children go to school in the morning and don't get home till four o'clock. Maybe by the time you got to sixth or seventh grade in Afghanistan, you went to school that long—I don't know. As a kid, I didn't know what the older grades did. Our school only went to fifth grade. Anyone who got further than that had to go to another bigger school farther away. I knew only that we little kids started at eight and headed home around ten thirty A.M.

And during those few hours we had recess, too, which we spent in the large central courtyard. The boys played running games, hitting games, wrestling games, throwing games, and

....

jostled pushed
casual relaxed

other **rambunctious** sports. We girls used to play a twirling game called *bobo-jan*, which means "mommy-dear." Two girls would hold hands and spin around and around until they got dizzy and then let go and try to walk. Why was it called "mommy-dear"? I have no idea. Sometimes we played other active games, like hide-and-seek, but never with the boys. I don't remember girls and boys ever playing together in my school.

Mostly, we girls sat in the sun at recess and told stories and ate our bread. We all brought big flat loaves of freshly baked bread to school. That bread had such a flavor at recess, because we were hungry. Actually, it was good anytime. The American bread I have eaten is generally made from **refined flour, and it has an airy texture**. Back home we made rich, chewy bread out of whole grain. I loved hot bread, fresh from the *naan-bayee*. *I* preferred that bread to meat, to kebabs, to anything. It tasted that good. Anyway, that's what all of us ate at recess.

A handful of students from wealthier families also came to school with a few coins clinking in their pockets. They spent their money at the school canteen, buying such snacks as salted chickpeas **marinated** in vinegar or *simian*, spicy-hot noodle-shaped pretzels. The canteen didn't sell drinks of any kind, but we all brought water bottles from home and drew fresh, cool water from the well in the middle of the courtyard.

As it happens, just about the time I started school, a bigger event occurred, but I was not aware of it. The Communist government of Afghanistan fell from power, and mujahideen took over the city. The mujahideen were the rebels who had

....

rambunctious wild and noisy

refined flour, and it has an airy texture flour that has been processed by machine, and is very light

marinated soaked

been fighting for twelve long years against the Soviets and then against the Communist Afghan government, which the Soviets left in power after they withdrew from the country in 1989. The mujahideen, however, were made up of many groups, and once they took over the city, they began to fight with one another. One group took control of a mountaintop in Kabul and, from there, fired down at its enemies in the various surrounding neighborhoods. Another group **made its headquarters** outside the city and launched rockets at night. Most of these rockets landed in other neighborhoods. We heard them, but we didn't worry about them too much. It was just part of life. Some days, however, were "bad rocket days," and then the schools would be closed. Or sometimes, during the day, we started to hear too many rockets, or the rockets sounded like they were coming closer and closer. On such occasions the teachers would say, "Go home, children. We'll **pick this up again** when things get calm." In short, school was sporadic— open some days, shut on others.

Still, when I was in first and second grade, I did not spend my days living in fear. There were exceptions, of course. Once, we heard that a rocket had landed directly on a school and killed some children. It wasn't in our neighborhood. It was on the other side of the city, in a neighborhood called Shar-i-nau, but we were scared that day, and when the teachers released us, we went home eagerly.

But the next day we had more or less forgotten about the school that got bombed in Shar-i-nau. There we were at our

....

made its headquarters put its military officers in a building
pick this up again start over

own school again, struggling over benches and then later assembling in rows to listen to our teacher. I loved school in part because I got to play with so many other children my own age, children whom I saw only at school, because they were not related to me. That's how it was in Afghanistan, at least for children: You spent most of your time with your family and your relatives.

In fact, when I think about it, that's what I really loved about school in general—the glimpse it gave me of a world beyond my compound and my family network. In first grade we merely learned the alphabet and the numbers, and I enjoyed that well enough, but in second grade school became something more for me. It became a place of wonder. In second grade we began to learn about the world. We had no books, just a teacher, but she was a wonderful woman. She wore a long colorful dress with a small hand-embroidered head scarf. Outside the school grounds, she replaced this with a bigger white scarf known as a *chadar-namaz*, a "prayer scarf." She was slender and very tall, and we children **took great pride in her height**. The taller she was, the grander she must be, we felt. Standing next to her at the chalkboard, we felt like ants, and that pleased us immensely.

What a wonderfully sweet woman she was—such a sweetheart! She told us stories about her own school days. She told us of the **ambitions she had nursed** in high school, of going abroad to study. She told us that when she attended school, she and her schoolmates wore Western-style dresses and went about in public bareheaded, which was no longer

....

took great pride in her height liked that she was tall
ambitions she had nursed goals and dreams she had

allowed now that the mujahideen held power: In public women had to cover their heads with a scarf. She told us about her wicked stepmother, who always tried to **douse her ambitions**. When she brought her report card home, her stepmother would glance over it and sneer, "Oh, so you're first in your class, I see. I suppose you think you're special." She told us she never got congratulated for anything she did, but she persevered, giving herself her own congratulations, and she told us we must also hold on to our **own sense of self-worth** and never succumb to anyone's sneering, scoffing, and **denigration**. I don't even know that lovely woman's name. We all just called her "Ma'lim Sahib," which means "teacher-sir." She filled our minds every day with the most astounding information. She put it in the form of stories. Even when it wasn't actually a story, she told it that way, because she knew that stories keep children interested and **agog**. Her storytelling got us to sit quietly and listen and forget about making mischief.

At that time I was just starting to wonder what lay beyond the limits of my own experience. I was pondering the big questions—the world, the skies, the universe. I remember one day our teacher astounded us with the news that the world was not flat, but shaped like a ball. That was so interesting to me! She told us, too, that there were other countries in the world, quite different from ours. The idea of other countries, other people different from us, wearing different kinds of clothes, living in different kinds of houses, speaking

---

douse her ambitions discourage her
own sense of self-worth pride in ourselves
denigration unkind words
agog excited, eager

different languages—this dazzled me and filled my mind with possibilities. I received her words like a desert receiving rain, just drank them in, drank up her stories.

At home I had often wondered what the sky was like. I pictured getting a long, long ladder and climbing up to the sky and feeling it. What would it feel like? I wondered. Would it be soft, hard, shiny, smooth, or what? And what if you could break through the shell of the sky? I **mused**. What if you could poke your head through the hole you broke—what would you see?

What was on the other side of the sky?

And then I went to school, and the teacher told us, "No, the sky is not like you think. It's not a ceiling. It vanishes as you come close to it. You could climb up toward it forever and ever, and you would never reach the sky." The idea of such a universe **swept me away with its majesty**.

Then she told us about the stars. She said the stars, which seem so small, are actually bigger than Earth itself. They only look small because they're so far away. Wow! After that I would often go out at night and stare up at the sky. I would think, *Okay, then. Let's see. If those twinkles are bigger than Earth, how very far away they must be to look so small!* What a universe this must be, to contain *such* distances. And what if you could travel to those stars and look from there, beyond, beyond—what would you see *then*? Just how far did the universe go? And where it ended, what was on the other side?

....

mused wondered

swept me away with its majesty amazed me

Every day I **hungered for** school, hungered to get there, hungered to hear what our teacher would teach us next! And that hunger was my downfall, for it made me careless—just for a few minutes, but that's all it took: **a single careless moment.**

---

hungered for really wanted to go to

a single careless moment one minute when I was not careful

BEFORE YOU MOVE ON...

1. **Conclusions** Reread pages 41–43. Farah rarely left home in Kabul. What does this show about her life there?

2. **Paraphrase** Reread page 56. Farah asked: "What was on the other side of the sky?" What does this mean?

LOOK AHEAD Read to page 68 to find out what happens to Farah that changes her life forever.

THE SHORTCUT

On that **fateful morning** I woke up and felt the sun in my eyes.

Now, Kabul is always sunny in the summer, and we did go to school in the summer there—our vacation came in the winter.

But I always got up before the sun had climbed above the mountain that **loomed** to the east of our compound. That light shining in my eyes told me I was late. I sat up and listened and did not hear a sound. For some reason, everybody in my house had overslept. It was eight o'clock. Class had already started, and I was missing precious minutes of my teacher's stories.

I jumped out of bed. In Kabul a schoolgirl wears a black dress with white stockings and a white head scarf. I threw on

....

fateful morning morning when my life changed
loomed rose

this uniform as quickly as I could. I didn't have time to pull on the stockings. They were too much trouble. Instead, I put on a pair of traditional white ankle-length pantaloons. I don't remember if I washed my face or not—probably, I splashed some water on it and said to myself, *That's good enough*. As for my long hair, I didn't have time to comb it. I just left it **tangled and unruly** from sleep, grabbed my school box, and rushed out the door, **forgoing** my usual morning bread and tea—I had no time.

Outside, I saw no other schoolchildren making their way down the road. They were all in school already.

And so I thought, *I'll **take a shortcut** today.*

By veering off the paved street and cutting across an overgrown brush-filled field directly to the main road that led to my school, I could save two or three minutes. I think most people knew to stay out of this particular field. Perhaps the grown-ups had told me to stay out of it, too, I don't know—a child forgets such warnings. I didn't see any warnings posted, but then, I wasn't looking. I was late to school, and that's all I could think about. I started across the field.

And then suddenly a fire flashed in my face and the earth seemed to move beneath my feet. I remember a shower of soil and then nothing.

I woke up on the ground, surrounded by a crowd, men and boys mostly, but a few girls, too. No women. They were all staring down at me with huge eyes. The color had fled from their faces. They looked **horrified**. Their lips were moving, but I could hear no voices. All I heard was a loud ringing in my ears.

....

tangled and unruly messy
forgoing without
take a shortcut *go a quicker way*
horrified very frightened

The sun blazed down on me, but shadows kept cutting across the light as people pushed their way into the ring of spectators. They just let me lie there for half an hour or more, I later learned. They didn't know what to do. They didn't know who I was. At that moment I didn't quite know who I was either.

I could feel a strange anxiety gnawing away inside me: I was late for school, late for school. I had to get up. But the sight of all the horrified faces buried that anxiety in chaotic panic. I tried to look down at my legs, but I couldn't. It was so confusing. I didn't know what had happened or why I couldn't get up. I felt no pain, no physical sensation at all, just **mental turmoil** and fear. Those horrified people standing over me were arguing. Was it too late? Was I dead? Should they lift me up? How should they do it? Yes, that's what they were disputing. The babble of their voices was beginning to come through the ringing now, as they loomed over me, shadowy faces and figures, sunlight twinkling through the shifting spaces between them.

And then at last I found my voice. "What happened?" I screamed. "Why are you standing there? Pick me up!"

But no one moved to help me. They just crowded against one another, jostling for position and craning over one another's shoulders for a better view of me. Such rage came over me then. I screamed at them. Oh, how I screamed! Even now, as I think about it, **I detect a coal of that very same anger still smoldering inside me**. All the years have not dissolved it away—that unreasoning and unreasonable anger. The crowd was huge and getting bigger. I wasn't wearing stockings. I

....

I could feel a strange anxiety gnawing away inside me: I felt worried and scared:

mental turmoil confusion

I detect a coal of that very same anger still smoldering inside me I am still very angry

remembered that suddenly. Stockings took too long to pull on, so I had just slipped on a pair of baggy pantaloons that morning, under my black school dress. And suddenly I knew that those pantaloons were gone. Nothing was left of them except the elastic around my waist. **That single fact flooded through me, overwhelming all my senses** for an instant. My trousers gone and people gawking at me! Thank goodness I was just a child, but even so—the shame of it. The shame!

At that moment a man leaned over me. I knew him. He was our neighbor. He happened to be passing by when he saw the ring of people in the field and said to himself, *I wonder what's going on.* He came over for a look and recognized me. That good fellow had a *patoo*, a large shawl that Afghans wear over their shoulders for warmth. With great tenderness, he spread that *patoo* over my shivering body.

It was he who sent someone to notify my family. My father wasn't home, but my mother came running, howling with dismay. **Her lamentation drove my panic to another level.** The fear she felt shot right to the core of me as well.

Meanwhile, our neighbor had hailed a taxi. He and the taxi driver rolled me onto the *patoo* and lifted that blanket by the corners. That's how they moved me from the ground into the taxi. I don't know what would have happened if that neighbor had not come along and taken charge. I don't know how long the crowd would have just left me there. That neighbor was one in a long series of people who have saved my life.

He and my mother got into the cab with me, and the driver

....

That single fact flooded through me, overwhelming all my senses That's all I could think about

Her lamentation drove my panic to another level. Her loud crying made me even more afraid.

took off. I still couldn't look down at my legs. It's not that I couldn't lift my head. I had the physical strength, but I lacked the will. I just couldn't bring myself to look. My mother was wailing "*Wai!* Dust on my head! My house be ruined! Where was I? What was I thinking, to let my darling daughter go out alone! *Wai wai wai!*" How she blamed herself! And how her wails kept **forcing upon me the fact** that something truly dire had occurred. I began trying to force myself to **sneak a glance** down there. And I couldn't do it. And I kept trying. Finally, I caught one quick glimpse, just one glimpse, and oh my God! That wasn't my leg anymore, it was just **meat**! Oh, the redness of it, the utter redness. *Akh!*

And still I felt no pain. When they lifted me out of the taxi, I screamed, but not from pain. I screamed because I knew. It was *knowing* that forced such sounds out of my throat: the horror of what had happened. When we got to the hospital, they loaded me onto a cart of some kind, rushed me indoors, and put me on a table. There, such a stench of blood and rot assaulted my nose, I couldn't breathe. I was choking. I said to myself, *This is it. I'm going to die. The end has come.* The scene before me turned black. I slipped out of the world and for some time, blessedly, knew nothing about anything.

Time passed. I suppose it did. It must have. While I lay there in shock, they brought my brother to the hospital, my older brother, the boss of us. I had lost a lot of blood. They gave me a transfusion of Mahmoud's blood. And so my brother became the second person that day to save my life.

....

forcing upon me the fact reminding me
sneak a glance look
meat bloody skin

When I **came to**, I felt as if a mountain had been loaded onto one of my legs. The weight—that's what the pain felt like: weight. Pure weight. I said to my mother, "What have you put on my leg? It's too heavy, get it off!"

My mother, poor thing, stripped away an army blanket they had draped over my legs, but this, of course, didn't help. The weight I felt was not the blanket, and nothing could lighten that load. My legs were quite uncovered now, and still the weight pressed down, slowly revealing itself as pain that pulsed and pounded.

Everyone was there around my bed, my whole family. I saw an aunt of mine who was **feuding** with our family. Even *she* had come. In Afghanistan, you know, when feuds spring up within a family, people might not speak to each other for months; they might refuse to visit each other's houses. But then at the holy festival of Eid they meet at someone's house and make up. So I was thinking, *Is it Eid? It must be Eid.* Otherwise, how had my aunt and my parents **reconciled**? If it wasn't Eid, something big must have happened. But only in a troubled and anxious way did I intuit that the "big thing" had some connection to the **mountain resting atop** my leg.

The next day, finally, they lifted me onto a cart to take me to the bandage-changing room. At that point I gathered my courage and took a long look at my legs. I saw that they were mangled. My family, running alongside my cart, now told me what had happened. "You stepped on a land mine." They told me the whole story. The doctors filled in the clinical details.

....

came to awoke
feuding angry, fighting
reconciled become friends again
mountain resting atop great pain in

By the end of that day I **had it clear in my mind**.

I was in the Kabul children's hospital. I don't know which part of the city that is in. As I said, I don't know much about the layout of Kabul. It was quite a big building, that's all I know. And I was in an enormous room, with rows of beds on this side and rows of beds on that side and a long aisle running between them, down the middle of the room, and wounded children lay in every bed. There were no private rooms. On my floor all the patients were children. I think the whole hospital was full of wounded children, but I don't know.

That first day I just slept, if you can call it sleep. I don't know if they gave me some sort of medicine or if **shock alone kept me oblivious**. In any case, I have no memory of those hours. The second day I woke up. After that I was awake every day, and by then my legs were unmistakably hurting. Every morning the hospital orderlies carted me to the "apocalypse." The apocalypse was the room where bandages were changed. After the first time, when they came to get me at that certain hour of the morning, I knew where they were taking me. I felt like an animal being hauled to slaughter. Changing the bandages was the most terrible ordeal. *Akh!* It could not have hurt more if they had thrust my legs directly into a fire. Every day the bandages had stuck to my wounds. To loosen them (and to kill germs, I suppose), the nurses doused my bandaged legs with alcohol, which felt like liquid fire pouring through my skin. Then they would *riiiiip* the bandages off—they weren't gentle. By no means were they gentle. I guess they felt

---

had it clear in my mind finally knew

shock alone kept me oblivious the pain made me confused

it was better to **get the thing over with** quickly. But I always knew what was coming, and **the apprehension constituted a terrible ordeal in its own right**. Then, when the time came to rip, they had to hold me down. I was so small then, and I couldn't stir below the waist, so I was easier to hold down than a wounded grown-up. They only had to grip my arms and push down on my **torso**. Usually, two strong adults could do the job. My mother—my poor, terrified, distraught, exhausted, and guilt-tormented mother—would give me her arm or hand to bite when they were ripping the bandages off. And I *would* bite—oh, I would bite hard! That's how I managed to stifle my shrieks, at least to some extent—by covering my mother's arms in bruises. She didn't have much fat on her, so biting her arm was like biting on bone. It hurts me now to think how I must have hurt my mother, but at the time I was lost in my own pain and nothing else existed for me. Now I have to say, oh, darling Mother, forgive me for what I put you through! And thank you for what you did. She's a good mother, this mother of mine.

I spent forty days in that Afghan hospital. The Afghan doctor was kind to me, but I don't know if he was a good doctor. There was no real way to tell. He had nothing to work with: no real medications, no tools, no medical equipment. That hospital did not even have bandages. Such was the story of Afghanistan at that time. The country had lost all its manufacturing. After all those years of war it had used up all its medical supplies. It had run out of money to buy anything from abroad. Thus, the hospital had no way to restock the supplies it used up or the

....

get the thing over with take the bandages off

the apprehension constituted a terrible ordeal in its own right just thinking about it made me feel pain

torso chest

equipment that broke.

My family, like other families, had to scramble around the city every day, trying to buy bandages in the bazaar to supply what I would need the next day. When they couldn't **come up with** proper bandages, the doctors and nurses had to wrap just ordinary cloth around my shredded legs. They didn't have **antiseptic creams** to put on the wounds before they wrapped them. They had only Vaseline, so that's what they smeared on the meat, just to keep the bandages from sticking. But it never worked. The bandages always stuck.

It's scarcely any wonder that during my forty days in that hospital, my right leg got infected. They changed all the bandages on the same table and didn't **sterilize it** between patients. When they brought me in, they set me on other people's blood and other people's gore; as soon as I was carried away, other patients had their wounds dressed in my blood and gore. It wasn't the kind of scene you picture in America when you hear the word "hospital." It wasn't that kind of hospital.

As for repairing my legs, they could not even attempt it. They didn't have the medical **prowess**. They knew how to douse a wound in alcohol and how to change a bandage. That was all. In that hospital they were just trying to keep me alive. They knew that every three months or so a German organization came to Kabul and chose a limited number of wounded Afghan children for treatment in Germany. The Afghan doctors were just trying to keep me alive until the Germans came. They knew that the Germans were my one and

---

come up with find

antiseptic creams germ-killing medicine

sterilize it clean the germs off of it

prowess knowledge or ability

only hope. If the Germans came and did not choose me, they would probably just have to let me go, but they were trying to keep me alive long enough to give me **that one chance**.

They talked to my parents about this possibility of going to Germany. "We can't treat Farah's wounds here," they confessed. "We don't have the skills. Her case is too serious. Let the Germans take her. It's her only chance."

When I heard about this conversation, I got scared. I was only seven at this time, remember, and I said, "I can't go alone. I won't do it. My mother has to go with me."

The doctors said, "That's not how it works. They won't take your mother, only you. You have to go alone."

Then that Afghan doctor spoke to me privately. He said, "Don't **fret** about this, my child. Go with the Germans. They're good people. You don't have to be afraid of them, and they're wonderful doctors. Why, they'll fix your legs so well that when you come back—just wait and see!—you'll be walking around in high-heeled shoes! We don't have the tools and skills to help you here, but in Germany, my child, they have experts. Experts! Yes, when they get finished with you, your friends will envy you. You'll be **the talk of the town**, strolling about in your high-heeled shoes. Go with the Germans, my child."

And I believed him. In those last days at the hospital in Kabul, he managed to **set my heart somewhat at ease**. I still remember how he patted my head and stroked my hair and calmed me down. He had a kind heart.

When the Germans finally arrived, that kindly doctor

....

that one chance an opportunity to be healed
fret worry
the talk of the town famous
set my heart somewhat at ease make me less afraid

pointed me out at once. "She's **our most serious case**," he said. "You must definitely take that one."

Well, the Germans took only those who were seriously wounded. If you had merely lost a hand or something and your wound was clean and looked to be healing, they wouldn't take you. In that sense, I was fortunate that my situation was so **grave**. I was awake when the Germans came. I was awake when they came to tell my doctor that I had been chosen. By then I was so happy to hear the news. The Germans were going to **fix** me. I was going to wear high-heeled shoes.

....

our most serious case the sickest patient
grave bad
fix heal

BEFORE YOU MOVE ON...

1. **Problem and Solution** At first, no one helped Farah when the land mine exploded. How was she finally helped?

2. **Irony** Reread page 68. Farah says, "I was fortunate that my situation was so grave." Why is this statement ironic?

LOOK AHEAD Read pages 69–85 to find out if the German doctors help Farah.

ALONE IN GERMANY

The Germans took about thirty of us Afghan children that time. Of them all, I was the most seriously injured, the closest to dying. I hardly remember anything about the journey from the hospital to the airport, just that every time they moved my legs, I screamed—and they had to move my legs **a certain amount**, of course, just to get me from my hospital bed into the airplane.

On the plane they gave me a row of three seats to myself, so that I could lie down. They fastened me down with belts and nested me in cushions to keep my body from jostling around. They attached me to **an intravenous morphine drip, which quickly wrapped me in a thick fog**. They did everything they could to make me comfortable.

....

a certain amount a little bit

an intravenous morphine drip, which quickly wrapped me in a thick fog a tube that gave me strong pain medicine and made me sleep

Even so, after the plane took off, while I was huddling there half unconscious, a foreign guy went by and just barely brushed against my leg by accident. It felt as if a fire had engulfed me from heels to head. How I shrieked! That poor man! He jumped back guiltily, thinking he had done something terrible. In truth, anyone might have brushed against me like that. It was nothing, poor fellow.

But after that the doctors put up some yellow tape to keep everyone else out of my part of the airplane. I remember those hours on the plane to Germany like something I might have seen while I was drowning in syrup. I woke up a little at the airport and had a vague sense of motion and commotion but only in the fuzziest and most dreamlike way. I just knew that they were unloading me from the airplane and into something else—a helicopter, as it turned out. When the helicopter took off, **its roar burst through the drug-induced fog surrounding me**—*kijagga, kijagga, kijagga!*—the loudest sound I had ever heard. I could hardly stand it. By that time, for some reason, they had stopped dripping morphine into my veins, so with each minute that passed, that roaring seemed to grow louder. By the time they got me into the German hospital, I was more or less awake.

It was night, and everything was very quiet. I was awake enough to see that this hospital was so clean, so still, so beautiful! **My heart opened at the sight of it, opened wide.** A feeling of relief, of luxury, even of gladness wove in there with the pain and confusion.

....

its roar burst through the drug-induced fog surrounding me I heard it through my confusion and sleepiness

My heart opened at the sight of it, opened wide. I felt much better seeing it.

They already had a room ready for me, a private room with a pretty bed, fluffy pillows, and many soft toys. Two nurses put me to bed and attached an intravenous tube to me again. I think they started **running glucose into me as well as morphine**, but otherwise, they just left me there to sleep.

I don't know how many hours I slept or how many days passed, but I woke up to see doctors, nurses, and medical personnel crowded around my bed, jabbering away in German—*blah di blah* and *blah blah blah*. I got alarmed. Who were these people? They were taking pictures of me, too, and some of them were sticking needles into me and taking blood. Others were poking at different parts of my body and examining me here and there. I had tubes stuck into me all over. They did all this while I was lying in that bed—they didn't **stir** me at all. Then sleep closed over me again, and the next time I woke up, they were gone and I was alone.

When I arrived in Germany, my bandages were caked with dry blood and stuck to my flesh. The time came to remove those bandages. I was awake by then and knew what was about to happen. My very bones tensed up as they moved me onto a **gurney**. But instead of tearing the bandages away, as the nurses in Kabul used to do, they set me in a tub of warm liquid mixed with some sort of brown medicine—iodine, I now realize. After the bandages were completely soaked and softened, they gave me some skin-thin rubber gloves to slip on. Then they gestured to me to take the bandages off myself. They knew that I could get them off better than anyone else, because no other person

....

running glucose into me as well as morphine giving me sugar water and a pain killer

stir wake

gurney cot; temporary bed

could possibly be as sensitive to my pain as I was. I understood their reasoning without understanding their words. They were so smart, those German doctors! I wondered why the Afghan doctors hadn't ever thought of this technique. I spent a long, long time in that warm liquid, peeling the bandages off myself, layer by layer, or at times just thread by thread. I didn't want to look at my flesh as I uncovered it, but I felt so grateful to the doctors for letting me do it this way. Their compassion made **my heart let go and made me surrender myself to Allah**.

I was happier after the old bandages had come off and my wounds had been slathered with antibiotic grease and dressed again in clean, antiseptic gauze. At times, in the days that followed, I slept what felt like normal sleep, rather than like getting muffled in cotton and stuffed into darkness against my will. Slowly, I discovered in myself **a capacity for traces of pleasure** because these medical people showed such lovingness to me and nursed me so graciously and brought me toys.

I have to say that the doctors in Afghanistan had a certain arrogance to them as a group. They acted like they were **of a higher station** than their patients. And the nurses? Even worse! You couldn't even talk to them—their station was so high above yours, they took any plea for attention as an insult. Once, when I cried and tried to turn away from an injection, the nurse just stalked away in a huff. "If you're going to fuss about this, you can stew in your infection," she said.

My mother ran after her pleading, "No, no, no, please don't be mad at my little girl. She's young, she doesn't know what she's saying, give her the injection. . . ." And at length the nurse relented and came back and haughtily gave me the shot.

The nurses in Germany were so different. They would sit with me at night, comb my hair, and put cream on my face. They would spoil me. In the morning they would pull the curtains aside and sing out cheerily, *"Guten Tag!"*—"good morning" in German. I learned a little of the language when I was there, although I have forgotten most of it now. They would say other things, too, like—oh, I don't know: "Are you feeling better, dear?" Things like that. It made a difference, just to have somebody notice you and take an interest in whether you were doing better or not. Going from the hospital in Afghanistan to this one felt like going from hell to heaven.

Still, I kept slipping in and out of consciousness in those early months, and every second or third time that I woke up, I found my room crowded with strangers in white uniforms **jabbering at one another** over my body.

As it turns out, the bone of my right leg had **eroded**. Dirt and blood had gotten in there. That's what they were talking about. After studying the situation, the doctors decided they had to remove the parts of my leg bone that had gotten infected. Otherwise, the infection would have spread to the rest of my leg and then to the rest of my body. In fact, the infection had already **reached a critical stage**, and there was no time to spare.

Strangely enough, my right leg, the less damaged one, had the more critical infection. So they removed my right knee and some of the bone just above and below that joint, and they fused

....

jabbering at one another talking to each other
eroded become very infected
reached a critical stage become very bad

my thighbone to my shinbone, holding them together with a metal rod that now extends six or seven inches into both bones. Each end of that rod is attached with pins to the bone. As a result, of course, I can no longer bend my right leg. I can bend my foot up and down because my ankle joint **remains intact**, but I can't bend my leg because I do not have a knee.

I vaguely knew that they were taking me to another room every so often. I didn't particularly know that they were performing operations on me there. They gave me strong medicine each time that **knocked me out**.

When they brought me back from the first operation, I was so **groggy**, I didn't know if it was night or day and whether one night had passed or ten. It meant nothing to me when more doctors showed up and stood around my bed, conducting grave conversations. They **examined me minutely**, studied my legs, and talked some more. A blanket obscured my view of my own legs, so I didn't know what they were looking at. They were talking in German, so I wouldn't have known what they were saying even if I could have focused on their words. But I was so heavily sedated that it all felt like a dream to me, a buzzing and humming without meaning.

I didn't know that they were talking about my other leg now. The left leg was more severely damaged. The land mine had shattered the foot bones and most of the shinbone. I guess this was the foot I had set upon the mine. There was no saving it. Some time later they took me back to the operating room. And again, I didn't know where they were taking me, and they

---

remains intact is whole; is uninjured
knocked me out made me sleep
groggy sleepy
examined me minutely looked at me closely

gave me **anesthetics** once I got there. When I woke up from the drugs, I was in my own room again, lying there with eyelids so heavy I could barely hold them open, a heaviness like a boulder filling my brain. Time passed, and I **eased back into consciousness**. But I didn't know what the doctors had done to me.

I only knew that I was feeling better. I was feeling no pain anymore. In fact, I was feeling nothing below the waist. The absence of pain allowed me to actually think clearly again, for the first time since the day of the explosion. I thought about my family back in Afghanistan. I began to imagine arriving home—how I would skip down the stairway from the plane, how I would run across the field to greet them, how they would clap and celebrate that I was back from Germany and all well again. Maybe they would have high heels for me, ready to wear. I wanted them to be red. Or would black be better? And what kind of shoes? I began to imagine different styles.

At that point the doctors had put a sort of frame over my left leg and a blanket over that. They put the frame up so that the blanket would not touch my leg. When I looked down (once I was awake again), that's what I saw: that tent-like dome of blanket. And for the longest time—I don't know how long, since time had no meaning for me in that hospital, especially in the early days—I never thought to look under the blanket. I just **gave myself over to fantasies** about returning to Afghanistan.

One day, however, I finally thought, *Let me see what they've done.* I lifted the blanket, looked down, and saw nothing at

---

anesthetics drugs that take the pain away
eased back into consciousness became more awake
gave myself over to fantasies dreamt

all where my leg should have been: just an empty space. Just absence. It was such a jolt. I felt as though an earthquake had given the entire building a shake.

About three months had passed since I'd gotten to Germany, it turns out. I don't know quite when, in all that time, they amputated my leg. No one told me about it when it happened. They just took me out, sedated me, brought me back, let me wake up; took me out, sedated me, brought me back, let me wake up. . . .

I had spent so many hours in blissful ignorance, living out my fantasies. Everything was going to be all right now, because I was in Germany. That's what I thought. They were going to fix my legs, and I was going to be just the way I used to be. I was clinging to that Afghan doctor's tale about high heels. That belief was the one thing that kept me going—that, and all the romantic stories the fantasy implied, about the life I would live, the love I would enjoy. **My heart was thrilling away to** those stories. For me, when I saw the emptiness below my knee, **the land mine exploded a second time**. *Oh my gosh, this is Germany*, I was thinking. *It's a good hospital, these are good doctors—why did they do this to me?*

It was then that I started to weep, all by myself in that hospital room. Quietly, though. And no tears came out. I had cried them all. I just sobbed and sobbed with eyes as dry as dust. And I kept thinking, *This is Germany! They're supposed to know how to fix a person's legs here. Why did they do this to me? If they know how to fix legs*, why didn't they fix mine?

....

My heart was thrilling away to I was happy thinking of

the land mine exploded a second time it was as if the accident happened again

No one heard my grief. I didn't scream or make a single sound. I kept everything bottled up inside me. After all, I had no one to share it with, you know. I couldn't even ask the doctors to explain their decision. They spoke German, and I spoke Farsi: We couldn't communicate. I had been so sure that I was going to walk again, that my life would **go back to normal**. I had spent so many hours imagining my return to Afghanistan, my family's surprise, the delight that would bloom on their faces as I ran to them across the airfield. I had spent so much time imagining myself whole again.

A single instant shook that fantasy apart. I saw a painting recently at the Art Institute of Chicago by a man named Picasso. That painting showed a woman shaken apart into a hundred pieces and then put back together, but scrambled, put together all wrong—a cheekbone here, a mouth there, the nose upside down, eyes in the wrong places. Picasso must have been through an experience like mine: How else could he portray exactly how I saw myself in that instant after I discovered that my leg was gone? But as I say, I didn't cry out loud at that time. I only turned the discovery over and over in my mind.

Why didn't they tell me?

That question kept hammering away inside me. They let me **build up my hopes**, and then everything broke apart for me. I felt like half a person now, alone with my emotions and confusions. I could no longer take pleasure in anything.

Eventually, my body started making tears again, and I cried every night. And one night those tears of mine attracted

....

go back to normal be the same again

A single instant shook that fantasy apart. When I saw my leg was gone, I felt sad again.

build up my hopes feel happy again

somebody's attention. My room was next to another one, and only a wall of glass separated these two rooms. Ordinarily, the hospital staff kept a curtain drawn across that wall to give both rooms privacy. But on that particular night the nurses had decided to pull the curtain back. I believe they thought that seeing another patient might make me feel less isolated and abate my loneliness a little.

And, in truth, I was feeling particularly lonely that night and crying particularly hard. The boy in the other room had just been through an **appendectomy**, and his mother was sitting by his side. She was crying for her son when suddenly she looked up and saw me. In the midst of her own grief that poor woman had the compassion to wonder about my sorrow. At such a moment as that, she **enlarged her heart** to include me in all her feelings about her son. And this, too, is the world. Whatever my story means, this is part of it, too. Again and again—even though this world is filled with **such indifference** and so much random cruelty—at a crucial moment some good person has **crossed my path** and taken the trouble to care about me.

Her name was Christina. When she saw my tears, she said to herself, *Who is that girl? How come she is crying? Why is she alone?*

She went to the nurse. "Something is wrong with the girl in the room next to my son's. I think she's in pain of some kind. She needs help. You should go check on her."

The nurses said, "No, no. She cries all the time. It's normal. She's just lonely. You see, she's from Afghanistan and has no family here."

....

appendectomy operation

enlarged her heart cared enough about me

such indifference many moments when it seems no one cares

crossed my path met me

Well! That very night Christina came into my room to comfort me. But I was still suffering from the discovery that my leg was gone, and I wouldn't look at her. I pulled the blanket up over my head, and I wouldn't take it off, wouldn't show my face. I never told her why I was so mean to her that day, and she never asked. I was mad at her because I was mad at everything and everyone.

She went home, but the next night, after visiting her son, she stopped in to see me again. And this happened every night after that, and **my heart began to soften**—toward Christina and then toward everyone.

After a week her son **was discharged**, but Christina kept coming to the hospital—not every night, but once in a while, just to see me. She brought me toys and flowers and cards and candy. She brought me art supplies. She spent hours by my bedside, and we drew together, and we showed each other what we had drawn. She introduced me to the joy of creativity. She brought me paper dolls and showed me how to cut out clothes for them. We played games together.

Meeting Christina was **a turning point** for me, because I had somebody now. I had *somebody*. That makes all the difference, you know. Even if your body is whole, your spirit can wilt. You suffer if no one knows you exist. So I always had my eyes on the door, waiting for this angel to reappear. *Will she come soon?* I was always thinking. *Will she come today?*

Eventually, Christina came to realize how anxious and restless the **anticipation alone** made me, so she gave me a

....

my heart began to soften I began to be nicer
was discharged left the hospital
a turning point an important event; a change
anticipation alone excitement of seeing her

calendar on which she marked the days she would visit and showed me how the clock moved so I would know what time to expect her. That helped, but whenever one of Christina's visiting days was approaching, time slowed down for me. If she was coming tomorrow, I found that today would not end. If she was scheduled to come later today, I had to tear my eyes away from the clock. I had to force myself to look anywhere else in the room and just wait. And when it seemed that two or three hours must have gone by and I could reward myself with a peek at the clock, I would **see to my dismay** that only one or two minutes had passed! Ah, **what torture** it was, waiting for Christina, but a torture mixed with pleasure, because when she finally did arrive each time, I thought I would burst with happiness.

Christina knew how to make clothes. She sewed outfits for me. I needed them, for I had **gone through a growth spurt** in Germany. My Afghan clothes no longer fit me. Besides, I liked wearing the same kind of clothes as the people around me. It made me feel like I, too, was a part of their wonderful world.

When I got a little better and could sit in a wheelchair, Christina asked the hospital for permission to take me out and about. At first she just strolled me around the hospital, but when the weather warmed up, she took me outside to the hospital grounds and let me feel the fresh air on my face. When I got even better, she took me out for ice cream and showed me a bit of the city. Then when I got completely better, she took me home to have dinner with her family. This happened toward the end of my second year in Germany.

....

see to my dismay feel sad
what torture how hard
gone through a growth spurt become taller

The first time the man came to measure me for a prosthetic leg, I said no. I didn't want a fake leg. The very idea of it **repulsed me.** He had brought a model leg just to show me, and I pushed it away angrily. "I won't wear that thing!" I snapped.

But a few days later he came back. "Look," he said, "wear it for a day. Just today, okay? Just try it."

I shook my head. He coaxed some more, and I kept refusing.

Finally, the nurse **flew into a rage** at me. "Do you want to spend your whole life sitting in that wheelchair? Do you think you can stay there till **Judgment Day?** You can't go on like this, Farah. You live in the world, girl! Now you get up out of that wheelchair and put on that leg."

Well, the nurse **cowed me.** I put on the leg just to stop her from yelling at me. I wore it for an hour that first day, just an hour, but I didn't walk on it. I couldn't, actually, because my other leg, the one with the steel rod, had not healed up yet. The doctors told me not to put any weight on that leg yet, so I could not, in fact, "get up out of that wheelchair," as the nurse demanded. All I could do was put on the prosthetic and get used to the feel and sight of it. But even that was a big step. In my mind I was getting up out of that wheelchair, and the mind is where it has to start. That German nurse did me a favor by scolding me. I wish I could tell her that now and thank her properly.

They didn't give me any solid food for about six months because it was too difficult to move me to the bathroom and because my injuries had also affected my digestive tract. They

....

repulsed me made me sick
flew into a rage became very angry
Judgment Day the end of the world
cowed me got me to obey her

put diapers on me and gave me nothing but liquids to sustain me. I drank water, juice, and tea from a cup and got all my other nourishment through that tube attached to my arm. That was how they fed me. The liquids kept me alive, but once I started to feel a little better, I wanted the taste of real food in my mouth—indeed, I started craving food. When the nurses hurried past my room with trays bound for other patients' rooms, I yelled after them, "Hey, you! In here! I want some."

I still didn't know their language fluently, **but an assortment of German words and phrases had filtered into my brain, and now they came flying out my mouth**. "Halt!" I would yell. "Stop!" It just killed me that they wouldn't give me any food. At lunchtime the aroma drove me totally crazy. And then I would shout in Farsi, "For the love of God! *Pleeease* give me some food. You're giving it to everyone but me. Take pity on me!"

And the nurses would poke their heads into my room and say, "*Nein, nein.*" They would tell me in German that the doctors would not permit me to have solid food yet. I did not have permission to eat. I would have to be patient. Someday I would eat real food again, they would tell me: someday.

Finally, the doctors said they could give me some food. They said I might be ready. The next morning, when the nurse came in with a basket of croissants, she said, "Do you want one of these? Or two?"

I cried out, "Give me five!"

But they gave me only two rolls, along with butter and jelly.

....

but an assortment of German words and phrases had filtered into my brain, and now they came flying out my mouth but I knew a few German words and quickly spoke them

Nein, nein. No, no. (in German)

And you know, I should have been transported, biting into them; but in fact, eating felt odd, and eating this unfamiliar food didn't quite **connect to the anticipation I had been building up**.

At lunch they brought me yogurt, the kind with fruit at the bottom. Oh gosh, I didn't like that at all—not at first. It wasn't like Afghan yogurt. Now I've grown to like it. They also brought me coffee-flavored chocolates. I couldn't stand those. I used to throw them away. Coffee—how could anyone think that flavor went with sweetness? But I grew to like mocha, too. Slowly, I gained weight. I got fat, like I am now. I must have weighed a hundred pounds. I gained the ability to sit up. The doctors came in wearing smiles and wrote in their notebooks. **They exclaimed at my progress** and congratulated one another. Everybody was happy about me. I was happy about myself.

A year and a half after I arrived in Germany, I was well enough to return to Afghanistan. My legs were as healed up as they would get. I felt no pain. I could stand up. I had learned to use my prosthetic, so I could actually walk. I could not skip or dance or wear high-heeled shoes, but I had **come to grips with** who I was now and felt comfortable with it. Really, I felt fine.

But they could not send me back just then, because the war in and around Kabul had intensified. By this time the mujahideen, the seven factions that had driven the Soviet forces out of Afghanistan, were fighting fiercely over the capital city. Indeed, various mujahideen factions were fighting over

---

connect to the anticipation I had been building up taste as good as I thought it would

They exclaimed at my progress They were happy I was better

come to grips with accepted

all the cities and towns of Afghanistan, and yet another army had risen up in the south, in the city of Kandahar, an army called the Taliban; but the fiercest battles were taking place in Kabul. Armies **dug into** the hills outside the city were fighting armies lodged within the city. Airplanes could not land safely at the Kabul airport. All flights had been canceled, at least temporarily.

The people in Germany had no choice but to keep me there and wait for a **lull** in the fighting. They discharged me from the hospital, however, and sent me to live in a hostel, with other children waiting to go home. This place was like a dormitory, with many beds to each room. The children came from many countries.

Living at that hostel, I got a feel for what it would be like to really live in this country, not as a patient, but as a citizen, a member of this society, walking about the city, going to school, eventually going to work.

I went to Christina's house and got to know more about her life. I could speak German pretty well by now, and we talked about many things. I didn't know that I was starting to forget Farsi—since I never had a chance to speak Farsi with anyone, I had no opportunity to discover that **certain words had slipped away from me**.

Living in Germany those last few months, I kept thinking, *Look how modern this place is. Look at the women, how free they are. They go to school. They work, doing every kind of job. Here, women can be doctors, bus drivers, television reporters, anything. Look at how*

....

dug into hiding in

lull break

certain words had slipped away from me I had forgotten my language

kind the people are and how peacefully they live together. I compared life in Afghanistan as I remembered it to the life I saw all around me in Germany, and I thought, *This is better. I want to have a life like this—getting educated, working, supporting myself, making my own choices.*

I didn't want to go back to Afghanistan, and yet I missed my family terribly. I felt their absence from my life as an ache that nothing could relieve. So, for that reason, I *did* long to go back to Afghanistan. In short, **emotions were clashing in my heart**.

And then came the news: The rockets had stopped raining down upon Kabul. Someone had arranged a cease-fire of some kind. At least for the moment a **commercial** airplane could get into the city. No one knew how long this calm would last, so I was told to gather my belongings at once.

I was going home.

....

emotions were clashing in my heart my feelings confused me
commercial passenger

BEFORE YOU MOVE ON...

1. **Cause and Effect** Reread page 73. The German doctors decided they had to remove one of Farah's legs. Why?

2. **Summarize** Reread pages 78–80. In your own words, tell why meeting Christina was a "turning point" for Farah.

LOOK AHEAD Read to page 104 to find out how living in Germany changes Farah forever.

BACK HOME?

‒❦‒

I had departed from Afghanistan **in a stupor of medicated pain**, knowing nothing of my surroundings except as images from a bad dream. I had not looked out the windows even once as we flew away. When I came back, however, I was sitting up and feeling quite okay. **My senses were alert.** I could pay attention to everything going on around me. The plane had many passengers, traveling for different reasons. I was just another passenger, lost in my thoughts, struggling with my mixed emotions, missing Germany already, looking forward to seeing my family, feeling **all tingly** at the thought of seeing my familiar childhood surroundings again.

Suddenly, the pilot announced that we had crossed the border and were flying over Afghanistan now. I looked down

....

in a stupor of medicated pain confused because of my medicine

My senses were alert. I was aware of what was going on around me.

all tingly excited

and saw nothing but mountaintops: pointy-looking black, blue, and gray rock puckered into endless jagged tip-tops sharp as nails. It was summer, but snow had already dusted most of those peaks, or else the snow had not yet melted from last year. Those mountains looked beautiful, I must admit. **They pulled at my heart and tightened my breath.** But the sight of them disturbed me, too. Where were the cities and towns of Afghanistan? Where were the villages, even? And did my country have no farms? When we left Germany, looking down from the air, I saw great green squares of **cultivated** land stretched side by side and end to end—as far as my eye could see in some places. Flying over Germany, I could make out ribbons of highway snaking across the landscape, and when I stared hard, I could even see **itty-bitty** cars flowing along them. Where were the highways of Afghanistan? As far as I could tell, Afghanistan had nothing built by people. As far as I could tell, my homeland was an empty, barren country. The sight of all that emptiness began to alarm me. I stopped looking. I huddled in my seat, clutching my hands together, feeling the anxiety swelling inside me like a harsh bubble.

All at once the plane banked into a sharp turn and at the same time began to drop rapidly. Planes coming in for a landing at the Kabul airport had to go through such maneuvers at this time because they faced the danger of missiles shooting them down. In order to minimize risk, pilots stayed at the highest possible altitude until they were directly above the airport and then descended as steeply as they could, in a tight spiral within

....

They pulled at my heart and tightened my breath. They made me feel happy and excited.

cultivated farm

itty-bitty small

the ring of mountains surrounding the city. When we started our descent, I could not see Kabul because it was directly below the plane. I could see no sign of any city until we had descended quite a bit. Then as the mountains rose up around us, I began to recognize them as the shapes I saw above our compound walls throughout my childhood. Moments later we bumped down onto the airstrip.

It was a sunny day. When I came out of the plane, I saw that the Kabul airport had just one landing strip, not many like the airport in Germany. Even on this single dinky little landing strip, weeds were growing from cracks in the concrete. Over to the side I noticed a hunk of twisted machinery that might once have been a helicopter, and farther in the distance I saw another couple of **ripped and gutted** tanks.

I came down the steps, holding on to the rail, and saw the terminal, a little building to begin with and now a falling-down, broken-looking ruin. Inside, it was just one large empty room with **unadorned** concrete walls. The windows had no panes, leaving the whole chamber open to the elements. The floor had no covering of any kind, no tiles or carpeting. It was bare cement. Every sound boomed and echoed and rang in there. The lights, few in number and weak, **barely diluted the gloom**. And I thought, *What is this? This airport is nothing! Just nothing! How could this be?* And I was thinking to myself, *Why is my country like this?*

We children returning from Germany were herded into several large vans. The same organization that had airlifted us

....

ripped and gutted destroyed
unadorned plain
barely diluted the gloom did little to change the darkness

out of the country now transported us to that same children's hospital from which they had taken me two years earlier. The sight of it made me **flinch and stirred up feelings of dread in my belly**.

Apparently, the families had been notified beforehand that their children were coming home, for when we clambered out of the van, we saw clumps of people waiting on the other side of the parking lot. Here a glad shout rose up, there a jovial clamor. With each outburst, one child from our group, and then another, and another let out a happy responding shout of recognition and went running or stumbling to his or her family. Steadily, the children melted away until only two were left, me and another girl. I thought, *Something happened to my family while I was gone.* The other girl must have been thinking a similar thought. We both stood there, our faces **growing longer and longer as apprehension tightened its grip on our hearts**.

But then—wait—who was that? Two taxis had pulled into the parking lot. My father and mother got out of one. My aunt, my sisters, and my brothers came out of the other. All of them had armfuls of flowers. I let out my own cry of joy and soon found myself swirled into the embrace of my family. So many had come to welcome me that there was scarcely room in the taxi. I was stuffed in among them like cotton into a pillow. I forgot to say good-bye to that one other girl who was with me. I forgot to look back to see if someone had come for her. I just hope her family came soon.

My family told me they had been delayed by traffic—it was

....

flinch and stirred up feelings of dread in my belly feel afraid

growing longer and longer as apprehension tightened its grip on our hearts becoming sadder as we grew more scared nothing serious, they assured me, nothing serious. Everything back home was fine, they said, just fine. They began to fill my ears with family news. My aunt, for instance, had borne another child since I left, a boy. God be praised; but he was too young to come to the airport. One of the cousins was staying home with him. But all this chatter felt like pellets bouncing off me. I felt separated from this life. **My head was still in** Germany, and I only wanted to tell my family about that gleaming world, but I didn't know how to begin.

Besides, I was already discovering something disturbing. I didn't speak Farsi very well anymore. I understood everything people said, but when I tried to express myself, my tongue felt clumsy and I often forgot some crucial word, and then I got stuck and couldn't finish my sentence. How could I **sink into the luxury of** being with my family again if I could not even talk to them?

Meanwhile, on our way through Kabul as I gazed out the windows, I saw one damaged neighborhood after another— walls broken down, buildings with shattered roofs, structures with missing windows, houses that looked deserted.

We came at last to our own compound, which was **intact**, and yet it looked so different. But it wasn't the compound that had changed—it was **my eyes**. I was looking at my family's hard-won home with German eyes. I stumbled through the gate, into the yard, and stared around me at the mud-brick buildings. How small and squalid the whole space looked, and how *enclosed*! Instead of making me feel safe—as they used to,

....

My head was still in I still thought about
sink into the luxury of enjoy
intact not destroyed
my eyes the way I saw it

as they still made my mother and no doubt my sisters feel—these high walls made me feel *imprisoned*. I felt as if I could not **draw a proper breath** in this compound. At once I began longing for space, for absence of enclosure, for freedom.

We went inside the house. My mother brought out a box and opened it to show me a single thick braid of my own hair. As a little girl, I used to have long hair, but they cut it off at the hospital. My mother saved that hair, however. After I went to Germany, she looked at my braid whenever she missed me. The box had a worn look from being opened and closed so many times. My mother also showed me the grease spot in the bedding, where I had hidden that stolen cookie, another souvenir she had treasured throughout these two years. We all laughed about that stolen cookie, and we cried about it, too, without quite understanding the meaning of our tears.

Even as we sat about chatting and crying and laughing, I was glancing about me with growing discomfort. Our rooms were painted in the loud, bright colors that Afghans like. This room was shocking pink, that one a vivid red, the one beyond it a bright blue. The rooms were all beautifully painted in accordance with Afghan tastes and customs. But to me, after being in Germany, these rooms seemed garish and cheap. Our home embarrassed me. I wanted the **subdued pastels** of Germany.

And the designs! In Germany the interior design had been simple and quiet—and that is what I still prefer. Even now, here in America, I would decorate simply if it were up to me, but

....

draw a proper breath breathe well
subdued pastels light colors

my mother likes floral patterns and bright colors. For her sake, we have glaringly colorful carpets and the brightest, busiest furniture we have been able to find. That's how our home in Kabul looked, too. We were sitting on bright red mattress pads around bright red Afghan rugs woven in the usual intricate Turkoman patterns.

And it wasn't just the colors and patterns that **shocked my senses**. We were sitting on the floor! We didn't have couches or armchairs. We had no tables. And soon my sisters brought out a long white cloth and spread it out—on the floor. It was time to eat, and our food would be served on this cloth—on the floor!

My mother served a festive meal that day, all the finest dishes in the Afghan repertoire—baked rice with raisins and carrots, fried turnovers stuffed with Chinese chives, white pudding flavored with ground pistachio nuts, rose water, and cardamom—but I had lost my taste for Afghan food. I didn't like what my mother had cooked. I wanted German food: roasted meat, dinner rolls, plain vegetables.

And I certainly didn't want to eat sitting on the floor. As for eating with my hands? From the same platter as my siblings? Yuck! I wanted a fork and my own plate. Nothing about Afghanistan sat well with me. It all felt alien. *Can this really be my home?* I thought.

My two years in Germany had changed me, you see. Of course they had! I was only nine years old! Those two years represented nearly one quarter of my life, and they were years **of earthquake intensity. They had stamped my tastes indelibly.**

....

shocked my senses surprised me

of earthquake intensity that really changed me

They had stamped my tastes indelibly. The years in Germany changed my tastes forever.

My family's way of life now seemed **primitive** to me.

And, oh my gosh, look at their clothes! They all wore baggy trousers, long shirts, head scarves and turbans, traditional Afghan outfits. I was wearing the clothes given to me in Germany. Of course I couldn't come back wearing the same clothes I had departed with. I had gone through that great growth spurt in Germany. At the age of nine I had almost reached my full-grown size. I was just about as big then as I am today. The old clothes no longer fit me.

But I also *liked* my German clothes, and I kept wearing them **for symbolic reasons**. As long as I wore those clothes, I was not really **"of" this alien country**. That's how I think I felt. Those clothes were my way of holding myself apart from Afghanistan. And, of course, in holding myself away from Afghanistan, I held myself away from the only Afghans I saw in daily life—my family.

To them, I'm sure, my alienation from all things Afghan seemed like snobbery, yet they never **held it against me**. Instead, oh, they lavished the kindest consideration on me, the most extravagant affection. Everybody else in the family slept on cotton-stuffed mattress pads on the floor, but I was given a cot. I didn't like eating with my hands? Well then, the family went out and bought me some silverware. In that household I alone ate with a spoon and fork from a plate of my own, while all the others gathered around the common platter and ate with their hands. And more often than not, I sat above them physically, for I alone sat on a chair.

....

primitive old; not modern
for symbolic reasons to remember Germany
"of" this alien country from Afghanistan
held it against me made me feel bad

In the morning they warmed up water and brought it to my bedside so that I could wash my face right there, even though the others all got up before dawn and performed their ablutions outdoors, with the customary cold water. All day long they catered to my every little whim as if I were some kind of star. Before my injury, when I was a little kid in this household, no one spoiled me. No one even noticed me much. I was just one more of the many children **underfoot**. Now they treated me as if I were some fragile creature in need of special handling. They did this out of love, I know, and because they had missed me, and because they were ever so glad to have me back, but beneath all their consideration I saw something else. I saw **pity**.

And I didn't like that. I didn't want pity. If less was expected of me, less was thought of me. That's how I saw it. I refused to **concede** that stepping on a land mine had made me any less than I used to be or could be. I refused to **scale back my ambitions** or reduce my expectations of myself. So I didn't like this life. I wanted to go back to Germany, only I wanted to take my family with me.

Of course, it was not just physical discomfort and cultural alienation that gave me bad feelings about Afghanistan. Constant fear played a part in my reaction, too. As a child, I used to hear a lot of gunfire. I thought it was normal. But in Germany I had grown unaccustomed to that sound. And besides, the war had heated up here in Kabul. Things had gotten a lot worse since I went away.

Once my family felt I was ready to handle more serious news,

....

underfoot in the house
pity that they felt bad for me
concede believe
scale back my ambitions lower my goals

they let me know that one of my uncles had **fallen victim to** the war. This uncle had one wife for several years, and he had some daughters by her, but she gave him no sons, so he married again. His second wife bore him several sons, and thus my uncle ended up with a large family. One day, during a period when rockets were raining down heavily upon the city and most people were staying indoors, my uncle's household ran out of food. Days passed, but the rockets kept falling. Finally, my uncle said, "Well, it's dangerous to step out of the house, but I have two wives now and all these children. If I don't go out and get some bread, my whole family will starve." So he made his way to the big Russian-built bread factory known as Seeloh. He was waiting at the bus stop with his arms full of bread when a rocket **randomly landed on that spot**, instantly turning both of my uncle's wives into widows and all his children into orphans. The younger wife remarried, but the older one remained a widow and lived with various relatives. One of her daughters later married one of my cousins, so she's living with her son-in-law now.

In short, gunfire and explosions rocked the city constantly at that time. On any random night—indeed, on most nights at any random moment—you might suddenly hear a boom and crash! The family was used to it. They knew what to do. In the middle of the night I would find myself woken out of a sound sleep by someone shaking me and muttering, "Get up! Get up!"

"What is it? What's going on?"

And booms would be resonating from somewhere outside the house.

....

fallen victim to died because of

randomly landed on that spot accidentally hit and killed him

And booms would be resonating I would hear the sound of falling bombs

"Get up! We have to go to the bathroom!"

"Why the bathroom?"

They didn't have time to explain. They just dragged me along. Eventually, I learned that we took shelter in the bathroom because it was a separate building behind the house and had no windows. The family considered it the safest place in the compound when rockets were coming in. Not a safe place, mind you, just safer.

Therefore, at least once a night, we huddled in that bathroom until the sounds of explosions faded away. My family **took this as** normal life, but it kept me in agony, and over the weeks it just ground my spirits down. I could not help **dwelling on the fact** that in Germany you never had to worry about rockets.

Days were relatively explosion free. The rockets poured in mostly at night. One time, though, my cousin and I were sitting in a window seat, trading gossip and telling stories. In Afghanistan the houses have thick walls to **provide insulation** against the winter cold and summer heat, which makes for windows deep enough to serve as seats. My cousin and I were sitting on cushions in one such window seat, **idling away the** time, when suddenly we heard that high whistling sound that a rocket makes when it is passing overhead. An instant later the entire house shook as the rocket landed right at the back of our yard, on the wall between our compound and our neighbor's: *krmpussssss!*

It was just about noon when this rocket burst upon us.

....

took this as thought this was a

dwelling on the fact thinking

provide insulation protect

idling away the wasting, passing

The explosion blew a hole in the wall between the yards and made the windowpane next to us bulge inward. I happened to be looking up at that moment and saw the glass bulge, like a sheet of something soft, like something made of plastic. If the window had exploded into fragments just then, it would have killed us both. But instead, after pushing the glass inward almost to the breaking point, the blast somehow reversed direction and sucked the glass back out. As it bulged back out, it burst into billions of glittering fragments right before our eyes, a powerful **jet of jagged shards** that sprayed across the yard. A few random fragments arced backward and hit us, but they landed harmlessly.

Of course, this whole event took only a second or two. By the time we realized that a bomb had landed in our yard, the whole thing was over. Dust was raining down outside, the explosion was in the past, the noise just an echo and a ringing in our ears. But the fear **slammed into us a half second later, and we reacted to that delayed wave.** Actually, I shouldn't say "we." Everyone else reacted. Not me. My parents, my siblings, my cousin—they all leaped to their feet and bolted for the hall, because they knew from long experience that if you couldn't get to the outside bathroom, you had to get yourself into the hall, the one place in the house with no windows facing the outside world. They had been through this drill dozens of times. They knew what to do.

I, however, froze. I couldn't move. My mother realized this and came running back for me. She grabbed me by the armpit,

---

jet of jagged shards explosion of sharp pieces

slammed into us a half second later, and we reacted to that delayed wave hit us and then we reacted to it yelling, "Come on, run, flee!"

I was trembling too hard to get up. She started dragging me toward the door. In trying to keep up with my mother, my foot caught on the rug, and I fell. I banged my elbow against the ground and cried, "Ow!" As in America, that's what people say in Germany when they get hurt: "ow" for "ouch."

But in Afghanistan when people get hurt, they say, *"Wakh!"* or *"Akh-Allah!"* So even at that tense moment, I reacted as a German, not as an Afghan, and nobody knew what to **make of** the sound I had just made.

Because in Farsi, as it happens, *ow* is the word for "water."

So my family thought I was calling for water. And what did my **solicitous** mother do? She started yelling at my siblings. "Get her some water, you lazy rascals! Can't you see Farah is thirsty?"

And my brother Mahmoud came running up with a big jug full of water. I was yelling, "No! Not that! Ow! Ow!"

And my mother, still misunderstanding, began scolding my brother: "What's wrong with you? Do you think she wants to drink it out of that great big jug! That's not how they do it in Germany! Pour it into a glass for her! A glass!"

And I was all red with frustration and still yelling, "No! You don't understand. Ow!" It made me angry that they thought I would **issue spoiled demands** and expect special treatment at a time like that—and it made me angry that my mother would **cater to my airs** if that's what she thought them to be. That wasn't me at all. How could they misjudge me like that?

....

make of think about

solicitous caring, helpful

issue spoiled demands be so rude

cater to my airs accept my rude ways

Well, finally, I managed to get across that I was merely trying to say, *Ouch, I hurt myself.* At that my mother **renewed her efforts** to get me into the hall, even though that was pointless. If a follow-up bomb had hit our house, we would all have been dead whether we were sitting in the front room or cowering in the hall. This bomb had actually landed in our neighbors' yard mostly, but the neighbors happened to be in rooms on the other side of the house. Their chickens got killed, their house sustained a little damage, but our neighbors escaped injury.

After we sorted out what had happened, we laughed a lot over that episode. *Ow! Ow! Get her some water, you rascals!* We weren't laughing at the time, but we laughed later. You have to take your laughs where you find them. It's good to laugh when you can.

Throughout this time, the streets were full of soldiers **skulking about** with guns, loyal to various commanders. **You had no idea who served whom.** Sometimes they burst into people's houses and took over, although, as far as I know, this never happened on our street. More often, if the soldiers came across an abandoned house—and so many houses fit that description in Kabul at this point—they swarmed in, claimed the place for themselves, and turned it into one of their encampments. Barracks of this type had sprung up all over the city, in all the neighborhoods. On some streets behind every third or fourth door was a compound bristling with soldiers, and you never knew which ones.

....

renewed her efforts tried again

skulking about sneaking around

You had no idea who served whom. No one knew who a soldier was fighting for.

You didn't hear many gun battles on the streets. By day the soldiers patrolled their own neighborhoods and kept out of neighborhoods controlled by others. As twilight approached, these soldiers hurried to get indoors, and there they cowered and watched the skies, because they faced the same problem as the rest of us.

Rockets.

Even in these conditions, my father went to work every day. He still made custom clothes for special clients and for people he knew and cared about when they had weddings coming up or other special occasions. But in a larger sense my father's business had changed. Over the last two years it had grown so much that you could not really call him a tailor anymore. No longer did he buy bundles of secondhand clothes to use as parts. Now he designed and produced **ready-made clothes from scratch**, in a workshop of his own, with ten apprentices. He had developed into a clothing designer and manufacturer, **producing goods in quantity**. He made what people in Kabul called "maxi" dresses, women's garments with long full skirts. He made men's suits, too, as well as jackets, vests, and winter coats. He cut out the parts, and his apprentices sewed them together according to his directions. You could find his products in stores all around Kabul, and they sold briskly, for they were every bit as stylish and sturdy as garments imported from abroad but were so much cheaper. My father had **his eyes on expansion**—on increasing his line, adding designs, acquiring more sewing machines, and opening another

....

ready-made clothes from scratch clothes that were ready to wear and made from new materials

producing goods in quantity making large amounts of clothing

his eyes on expansion plans for his business to grow

workshop. Even as war raged throughout the city, he was laying big plans and going to work every day, and we always watched him leave the house with our hearts in our throats and we worried about him until he came back home at night.

We had no sense that the war had any particular "direction," no sense that anyone was gaining or losing ground, no sense that it would make any difference if anyone did gain or lose, no sense that the war could possibly **move to any conclusion**. Different armies held different parts of the city, that's all we knew. **Word was going round** that the Taliban were still approaching from the southwest, from Kandahar. They had gotten past Ghazni and were now advancing on Kabul. The mujahideen, while still fighting one another, were trying desperately to hold off this new force.

We had no special feelings about the Taliban, pro or con. They were just another army. People like us were just caught in the middle, trying to avoid taking sides, wanting no part of the battles, trying merely to survive, work, live. We had no sense of a climactic moment or turning point coming up. One day's battles melted into the next day's. War was just **the unremitting background against which** daily life went on.

And everyday life did go on. It had to. No one had a choice about that. People had to go out and shop when they ran out of food or other necessary supplies. People had to go to work, when they could. They had to make a living somehow. But we women and girls didn't go out much, not with the war raging and the streets crawling with random soldiers. And no one

....

move to any conclusion end

Word was going round News was spreading

the unremitting background against which constantly continuing as

was going to school much in those last days of mujahideen rule, neither boys nor girls. On most days schools were closed, because nowadays every day was a "bad rocket day."

I could not **reconcile myself to** this way of life. I talked to my father about it. I said, "This way of life is not for me. I don't want to live like this. I want to leave Afghanistan." I told him about Germany and all that I had seen there.

And what could my poor father say? He worked **his heart out** and risked his life each day to make a life for his family. "Well, my child, this is the world," he would say with a sigh. "We just have to live in it and get by as best we can."

I kept demanding to know why we Afghans had to be like this—fighting all the time, building nothing, **clamping down on** our own freedoms: What was wrong with us? My father had no answers. All he could do to **alleviate the rigors of my life** was to give me sewing lessons when he had the time. He hoped that this distraction would take my mind off the war. Later in life I had good reason to look back on those lessons with gratitude, but at the time I just plied my needle in silence and dreamed about Germany.

Four months after coming home, I was still wearing my German clothes, but my resolve was weakening. When I first found myself in Germany, I knew great loneliness because I could not communicate with anyone and because I had no family or friends there. Here in Kabul, I suffered from loneliness again, but a loneliness of my own making. I had family, but I would not melt in with them. I refused to fit in.

....

reconcile myself to accept

his heart out very hard

clamping down on taking away

alleviate the rigors of my life make me feel better

Gradually, however, I began to see that holding myself apart from Afghanistan was not getting me any closer to Germany. In fact, it did me no good at all. Instead, it cut me off from **the only source of warmth and nourishment available to me in this life**.

I began to say to myself, *Well, this is where I live. Germany was a dream and a fantasy. I have to let go of that now. I have to accept reality. I am going to live the rest of my life in Afghanistan, and I have to make the best of it.*

One momentous day I concluded, *It's over.*

I went to my father and told him, "I will put away my German clothes. From now on, I am going to dress as an Afghan girl again." And although this was the moment when **my defeated spirit surrendered to grim reality,** it also represented the moment when I opened myself to my family again and let their warmth and love back into my life. My older sister, Niloufar, had extra clothes that would fit me, and I told my parents she had agreed to let me share them.

My father would not hear of this. His prodigal daughter was really coming home to him at last. He said, "No, you need clothes of your own. I will make you a whole new wardrobe."

In Afghanistan new clothes have importance. One of the things we do at the holy festival of Eid, for example, is get new clothes, so that we can feel like we are starting over, with new hopes and fresh dreams. This was the feeling of renewal my father wanted for me: green hopes, new dreams, a fresh life.

He told my mother, "Get the boys. Go to the fabric bazaar.

....

the only source of warmth and nourishment available to me in this life my loving family

my defeated spirit surrendered to grim reality I knew I would never return to Germany

Get her all the fabrics she wants, whatever she wants, as much as she wants. Bring it home, and I'll make new clothes for my daughter."

Well, I went to the bazaar with my mother and my brothers. We spent the morning looking at fabrics—**fingering this one and that one**, discussing colors and styles and how much I would need of each item. **Using the language of** clothes, we talked about a new life for me. And that day we bought a lot of fabric, yards and yards of it. Having made my decision, I felt relieved and relaxed now. Something wonderful **uncurled and began to sprout in my heart**.

Far away, in some other neighborhood, guns were going off and cannons were booming. I scarcely noticed it, just as I scarcely noticed the growl of traffic or the blare of horns or the background hubbub of the bazaar. I had grown accustomed to the sound of war. It was just city noise to me. I had become an Afghan girl again.

....

fingering this one and that one touching all of them
Using the language of Talking about
uncurled and began to sprout in my heart made me feel hopeful

BEFORE YOU MOVE ON...

1. **Summarize** Reread pages 90–93. How did Farah show that she was no longer comfortable in her country?

2. **Author's Point of View** Reread pages 102–103. What did Farah realize that helped her accept her life as it was?

LOOK AHEAD Read pages 105–120 to find out what happens to Farah's father and sisters.

LOSING MY FAMILY

~~~~

We started home at last, glowing with good feeling from our morning's shopping expedition. But when we reached our own street, we saw a crowd milling about, right where our house should have been. **Dread filled our hearts**, because we knew at once. Yes, some instinct takes over at a time like that, and you draw on deeper ways of knowing. "A rocket hit our house." My mother and I both said it at once.

We pushed our way through the crowd, and there it was: Our worst fears had come to pass—our worst nightmare. I noticed the jumble of shattered tree parts littering the yard. That's what I saw first. Next, I just **registered a general impression of chaos and ruination** everywhere.

Then I saw our house: reduced to nothing but piles of rubble

....

Dread filled our hearts We were afraid

registered a general impression of chaos and ruination saw confusion and destruction and broken glass.

And then I saw the bodies.

The bystanders who had come to mill and gawk had spread shawls, blankets, whatever they could **muster up at such short notice**, over the bodies of my **martyred** father, my poor sisters. So I didn't really see them. I saw shapes.

There at the scene, I didn't look at my father's face. I was too afraid. I just stood there frozen, feeling dry and drained. My throat felt stuffed with something huge. I couldn't cry. Or didn't, anyway. I just stood there trying to swallow.

My mother, however, ripped the scarf from her head and began to tear her hair out by the roots, handfuls of it. She began to tear out her hair and scream.

Shocked to my bones, I yelled, "Don't, Mother-darling, you'll hurt yourself! Don't tear at your hair!" But she didn't seem to hear me. She didn't seem to know where she was. Women came swarming around to grab her arms and try to stop her from hurting herself, and she struggled in their grip **as if possessed**, her eyes blank and her long hair coming out in bunches.

My grief at that moment gushed entirely for my mother. I panicked on *her* behalf. I worried for *her.* I forgot all about myself, forgot all about crying. There in the presence of my father's corpse and my sisters' lifeless bodies, I was conscious only of the terror and panic I felt for my mother. The way she tore her scarf from her head! An Afghan woman should wear a head scarf at all times—no strangers must ever see her

....

muster up at such short notice find quickly
martyred honored
Shocked to my bones Surprised and afraid
as if possessed as if an evil spirit was in her

hair! And my mother had always been so **scrupulous about her modesty**, but now she **had catapulted beyond all such considerations**. She snatched that head scarf off, she ripped out her hair, she tore her scalp and drew blood. Then she flung herself upon the ground. And they—the strangers who had come around—pulled us back from that scene by force, murmuring, "Don't look. Everything will be fine." They murmured those untrue words. Everything would be fine! "Don't look. God is gracious. Don't look." They led us away. It felt like a dream at the time, all noiseless and slow, and when I look back, it still appears to me that way: as a strange event, unfolding in slow motion, behind a pane of thick, dark glass. The screaming, the **turmoil, the hustle and bustle**, the sense of wildness—it all recedes from me into a dream as I am led away from our devastated house by strangers.

They took us to my uncle's house, my mother's brother. He lived fairly close by. Come to think of it, maybe it was my uncle himself who took us there. He seemed like a stranger at the time. Everyone except my mother looked like a stranger that day.

Now that I'm talking about it, I wonder what happened to all the cloth we bought in the bazaar that morning. My new clothes. What happened to all that fabric? I have not thought about it until this moment. We must have dropped it there in the street, outside our compound. Someone must have gotten away with it. Well, I hope it gave them satisfaction. We had no further use for it. Who would make new clothes for me now that my father was dead?

....

scrupulous about her modesty careful to be polite

had catapulted beyond all such considerations was not even thinking about being polite

turmoil, the hustle and bustle confusion, the speed

When we got to my uncle's house, it was full of relatives. Everyone was there, waiting for us. Somehow all of them had already heard what had happened and had gathered. I don't know how the news spread so quickly. I can only suppose that the rocket must have struck our house many hours before our return home. The news had reached everyone who was home to receive it. We didn't hear about it because we were in the bazaar, moving about. No one knew where to find us.

My mother fainted at my uncle's house. The sight of her **collapsing unleashed my wails at last**. But the moment I opened my mouth, someone gave me a hard slap across the face and said, "Your crying will **distress** her even more. You stop that crying and control yourself!"

Most of my relatives stayed close to my mother that night. They clustered around her and held her and tried to comfort her. How she fared, I don't know, because they shut me up in another room. I spent the night alone, a strange night, a night in which I had no thoughts that I can remember and no feelings. I just lay on the ground, curled up, inert, stunned, unable to feel, no different than a stone.

Finally, the morning came, but the light seemed no different than darkness. It was like waking up from a nightmare only to find oneself still in a nightmare, and it was the same nightmare. The horror of yesterday merely became the horror of today. Everyone gathered around to **solace me**, all my girl-cousins, but I could not receive their sympathy or cheer. I snapped at them to leave me alone. Poor things had come to console me,

---

collapsing unleashed my wails at last falling made me cry finally

distress upset, worry

solace me make me feel better; comfort me

and I ungraciously lashed out at them. I told them to forget about me.

In those first few days after the catastrophe I was so dazed, I scarcely registered the existence of a world outside the turmoil of my own heart. I could hardly make out my brothers, my cousins, my uncle's household. The conversation around me sounded like the meaningless buzzing of insects. How much less, then, could I **sort out** what was going on in the city as a whole and in the history of my country? If you're locked in a noisy room, you can't tell if the rest of the house is quiet or not, if the streets are deserted or filled with rioting mobs.

Only in retrospect do I understand that my father's death was just one part of a momentous event that befell Afghanistan in that last week of September 1996. Three or four days after the rocket killed my family, the mujahideen slipped out of Kabul and retreated north, leaving the capital city to the Taliban, that terrible army of big-bearded boys. It was all part of the same cluster of events, the Taliban's final battle for Kabul. I knew of this event only dimly. Certainly, I knew nothing of its significance.

Others understood more about it. **The sense of crisis gripping my uncle's household stemmed** from more than my father's martyrdom. With the city in such turmoil, with no one sure what would happen next, no one dared to make suitable arrangements for our loved ones. A group of men hurried to our house, dug them out of the rubble, bore them to the cemetery, and buried them in haste. They told me to stay

....

sort out understand

Only in retrospect Only when I think back

The sense of crisis gripping my uncle's household stemmed The fear and worry in my uncle's house came

home. The cemetery was in the city, but you could not drive right up to it; you had to park far away and walk to the grave site—**an arduous** walk, people said. They told me that with my fused knee and prosthetic leg, I could not possibly make it from the car to my father's grave to see him lowered into the earth. Actually, I could have walked that distance. I proved it later. But no one gave me credit. They thought of me as the poor cripple. I suppose they thought I might slow them down if trouble broke out and they had to run for it. My mother and brothers went to the cemetery that day, but not me.

The **services that sanctify and honor the dead** were not performed for my beloved father and my cherished sisters. We had to forgo the rituals that would have given closure to our grief. We could not have the funeral prayer conducted in the mosque. In other circumstances those prayers would have drawn hundreds of mourners. So many people knew my father; so many would have wished to pay their last respects to him and to my sweet sisters. But none of these things were done. Everybody was too frightened, too shattered, and with the Taliban coming, the danger to our own lives had suddenly **ratcheted up to crisis level**.

I do remember the day the Taliban actually entered Kabul. My shock and confusion had lifted enough to let the bigger world into my consciousness. And what entered into my awareness that day was the nothingness, the eerie silence. No guns went off for once, no bombs sounded, no rockets fell that day. You didn't hear the sound of children playing. You didn't

....

an arduous a very difficult

services that sanctify and honor the dead holy burial ceremonies

ratcheted up to crisis level become greater

hear cars. You didn't hear dogs or donkeys or chickens, not even the hiss of bicycle tires. If you peeked out your door, you saw no one on the streets. If you looked out from an upper window, over your compound walls, at the more distant streets, you still saw nothing and no one.

The whole city was closed that day. Everybody knew the Taliban were coming, so no one went to work. Even hiding in our compounds, however, we felt the atmosphere of terror. The very air somehow felt wild and frightening. Everybody was just waiting and holding their breath.

Four years earlier, when the mujahideen had entered the city, their armies poured through the bazaars, **looting** stores, beating bystanders, and clashing with one another. I heard whispers now that people were afraid the Taliban might do the same thing. And indeed, there was some looting, supposedly, but it wasn't the Taliban who did the looting. This time gangs of lawless Kabul residents went roving through the richer neighborhoods, breaking windows, tearing open doors, and snatching whatever they could snatch. They thought they **saw opportunity in that moment between two regimes**. But the Taliban armies found them and silenced them; I don't know how.

Normal folks, which included most of the people of Kabul, locked themselves in their compounds and waited. For many days people went out only to shop, and even then, only if they were desperate—if they needed food, for example, or if they needed medicine. Most came back empty-handed because they could not find any open stores. I recall hearing that in

....

looting robbing; stealing from
saw opportunity in that moment between two regimes
were safe because there was no ruling party in power

our neighborhood one store did stay open, and that merchant tripled his prices. He made a lot of money until the Taliban had gotten such **a firm grip on** the city that more shopkeepers dared to open up for business.

Shut away in our houses as we were, we did not see any Taliban at first. We only heard them on the radio. They announced themselves. They said, "We are the Taliban, and we are here to stay." They broadcast their rules. Women could not leave their compounds without **male escorts**. If they did go out, even with escorts, they had to wear a *chadari*, a baglike veil that covers a woman from head to foot. For some reason, Western reporters always call this type of veil a "burqa," but in Afghanistan it is called a *chadari*. Also, everyone had to say *namaz*, the ritual Muslim prayer, at **prescribed** times. Men were forbidden to trim their beards. And so it went, their rules—on and on. The Taliban were just voices on the radio to us.

Then, by and by, we began to see members of the Taliban themselves. A few of them appeared on our streets and in our bazaars. Oh my God, they seemed like wild, alien beings, beasts from another world. They wore kohl, which is a black makeup, like mascara, on their eyelids, and they **sported** huge beards. They all wore big turbans.

Gradually, their numbers increased and increased, until they were everywhere. Even we women saw them, because now we could go out, as long as we wore *chadaris*. They became a normal part of our landscape, but they still looked frightening. You could tell at a glance which ones were Taliban, even from a

....

a firm grip on complete control over
male escorts men to guard them
prescribed the appropriate
sported grew, wore

distance, and not just because of their beards—for soon all men were growing their beards out **to avoid flogging**. Somehow the Taliban still stood out. Maybe it was the way they wrapped their turbans. Their clothing played a part, too. Their shirts were longer than the usual Afghan outfit, and they always wore dark colors. Maybe it was their **menacing swagger**.

In the end, it's hard to pinpoint what made them look so foreign and so alien. They just did. As awful and unnerving as **the chaotic reign** of the mujahideen had been, at least they seemed like Afghans to us, just brutal, lawless ones. Now we felt like we were in the grip of some strange force unlike anything we had ever seen in our country. Every glimpse of those Taliban men scared us. If we saw one on the street, we immediately wanted to change course, go some other way.

The four of us—my mother, my two brothers, and I—stayed with my uncle for two weeks. After that, with **heavy hearts**, we went back to our own house to sort through the rubble and see what was left. We used to have five buildings in our compound. Two were totally destroyed and one was badly damaged. We didn't feel safe entering it. Two buildings remained structurally intact. The blast had blown out all the windows, but the rooms still had ceilings and doors. Our chickens were still alive, clucking about the yard. We decided to move back in and live in the rooms that remained. It had gotten quite cold by this time, however, so we faced the problem of getting through a Kabul winter in rooms unshielded from the elements.

My brothers got busy nailing boards over the windows.

....

to avoid flogging so they would not be beaten
menacing swagger frightening way of walking
the chaotic reign the confused leadership
heavy hearts great sadness

These made the rooms dark, but we preferred dark to cold. They sifted through the rubble looking for clothes, pots, and other possessions we might salvage. All in all, we were living a primitive life now, but the problems of surviving from one day to the next kept us **preoccupied, distracting us somewhat from our losses.**

Meanwhile, the new rulers were making themselves known to the people of Kabul. Rapidly, we were learning that this was not just another mujahideen army, but something different. We heard about the floggings they administered to people who had broken their rules, especially to women they caught outdoors without male escorts or women they caught in public dressed— by their standards—immodestly.

At least in the days of the mujahideen, we women had the legal right to go out, go to school, and go to work, even if it was sometimes too dangerous to do these things. And women could go out wearing ordinary traditional clothes along with a head scarf and a neck scarf. And although, even in those days, some women did wear *chadaris*, they did so by choice—it was their custom. No one had to. The mujahideen disapproved of Western dress, and most of them had conservative standards; but within those limits, they allowed women to choose their own style of dress.

The Taliban put an end to choice of any kind. If they saw a woman without a *chadari*, they beat her with a stick or a rubber hose or the butt of a gun. They didn't go house to house, these Taliban. **I'll give them that much.** Unlike the mujahideen,

....

preoccupied, distracting us somewhat from our losses busy, helping us forget about our difficult lives

I'll give them that much. That was one thing that was good about them.

they respected the privacy of the family compound. But if they caught a woman on the streets, she was in trouble.

At first most women could not go out at all because they did not even own *chadaris*. A few rummaged around in their storerooms and found some old moth-eaten *chadari* their mother or grandmother had worn thirty or forty or fifty years ago, but most families had thrown their *chadaris* away.

Gradually, however, all of us who did not already own a *chadari* bought one. Soon, in any public place, you saw *chadaris* of every color—white as snow, sky blue, lemon-hued—pretty colors. The *chadari* sellers were going wild with joy. **This was their boom time!**

I rarely left our compound after the Taliban took control of the city. But one time, I remember, a family in our neighborhood invited us over for dinner, so I put on my *chadari*. Everyone else's *chadaris* fit them fine, but on me, because my nose is so flat, the **patch of mesh** you're supposed to see through pressed right against my face. I had to crumple up some paper and stick it to my nose with paste so that it would hold the *chadari* far enough away for me to breathe properly and see through the mesh.

Even then, as it turned out, I didn't know how to get about in a *chadari*. I couldn't walk in one very well with my prosthetic, and I didn't know how to see where I was going. That mesh at eye level lets you see only what is straight ahead of you. You cannot really look down at your feet, and you **have no peripheral vision**. There is a technique to walking

....

This was their boom time! Now they could earn a lot of money!

patch of mesh net, screen

have no peripheral vision cannot see what is on either side of you without tripping when you wear a *chadari*. You have to study the path ahead and memorize the landmarks, because as you move forward, the path disappears from view into the blind spot near your feet and on your two sides. If you see a curb coming, for example, you have to use your judgment as you approach it, as well as your memory, to figure out when you are there; and you have to feel for the curb with your toes, the way a blind man uses a cane. Otherwise, you can't know when you've come to the curb, and you fall off, or at least you find it hard to step off at the right place. All this must be learned; but when you have two injured legs and one of them is made of plastic, the technique is difficult to master.

For these reasons, once the Taliban **came in**, I rarely went out. Well, none of us women did. We had the boys do the shopping, or we pooled shopping trips with the neighbors, so that one group would shop for several compounds. That way each compound had to go out less often.

About a month after my father's death the Taliban announced that they needed more soldiers for their army. Every family had to give up its sons, they said. They were going to **sweep through the city, drafting** young men, teenagers, and even boys as young as ten or eleven. No one could hide from them, they warned. **Woe to** any boy who tried to escape their draft. Woe to any family who refused to open up when the Taliban forces knocked on their doors.

By this time we knew something else about the Taliban. They bore a special hatred toward Hazaras, my ethnic group.

....

came in took control of Afghanistan

sweep through the city, drafting move through Kabul, taking

Woe to They would punish

When it came to Hazara boys, they might not draft them, but instead might simply execute them.

My brothers could not leave the compound for fear of being caught by the Taliban. We did not even have intact walls protecting our privacy, for the rockets had blown our walls down in places. We lived in dread of those bearded bullies suddenly appearing in the gap where our compound gates used to be.

At that we were **no worse off than** our neighbors. They had sons, too. Most of us in the neighborhood were Hazaras. We were all **vulnerable**. One evening, therefore, we got together with our neighbors to discuss what we might do. My mother said that if my brothers were drafted into the Taliban's army, she would consider it a fate as bad as death. "Those people killed my husband and my daughters!" she wept. "And now they want my boys to go fight for them? I can't allow it! I would rather tear out my eyes than see my boys serving the people who killed their father!"

Our neighbors nodded, murmuring agreement. But what to do? We huddled around the fire, blinking back the tears the smoke drew out of us, **wringing our hands**. The wind hissed through the cracks between the boards. No one spoke. We were all lost in our thoughts.

Finally, a neighbor said that the boys had to **make a run for it**. They had to escape to Pakistan. There was no other way.

My mother agreed. "You boys are in immediate danger," she told my brothers. "You have to go right now. Farah and I

---

no worse off than in as much danger as
vulnerable in trouble
wringing our hands worrying
make a run for it flee; leave the city

don't matter, our danger is not immediate, we can come later. If we go with you now, we'll only slow you down—because who knows what it might take to get to Pakistan? Who knows if you'll have to climb mountains, swim rivers, cross deserts? You might have to go without food for days. Without water. You boys are young and strong—you can **endure such hardships**. You go on ahead, and Farah and I will come out when we can and we'll find you. Then we'll all be together again somewhere safe, **if God wills it**."

"And it's better if all our boys go at the same time," added the same neighbor. "All the boys together as a group—that's the way to do this. They can look out for one another, the older ones can protect the younger ones. Let them all head for Pakistan. That's where people go to escape Afghanistan. That's what I've always heard."

And we all said this sounded good. We had no idea what the plan actually entailed. Pakistan? It was just a name to us. How far away was it? We didn't know. How did people get there from Kabul? We had no clue. My mother had grown up in a village and spent her life in a compound. She had no sense of the world. I was barely ten years old. I knew how long it took to fly to Germany but not how long it took to walk to Pakistan, if walking was indeed the way to get there.

The neighbors had a little money to give their boys. My mother still had the gold jewelry she had bought, back in the days when my father was alive and making money. We found a friend who **had the necessary connections** to sell some of

....

endure such hardships survive these dangers

if God wills it if that is what God wants

had the necessary connections could help

that gold in the bazaar. He gave the money to my mother, and she gave it the boys: Mahmoud, who was sixteen then, and Ghayous, who was about nine.

They would try to board a bus for the city of Jalalabad, which lay about halfway to the border, and from there, who **could tell**?

My mother hugged her sons. I hugged my brothers. We all wept.

We held the Koran up to the **lintel** so they could pass under it as they went through the door, then we had them come back and pass a second time under the Koran, and then they passed under the Koran for a third and final time, departing from our house.

My older brother was holding my little brother's hand as they **set off** with the neighbor boys. We watched them go, a little band of boys, heading into the world on their own, with no one to protect them, no one to care for them except one another.

I never saw my brothers again.

Well, the weeks and months passed after that. We waited for some word from the boys, but what word could we possibly receive? We had no phone—there were no phone lines from Kabul anymore. The country had no real mail service anymore either; for the most part, only hand-carried letters could get through. What money we had **dwindled and dwindled.** With my father's death, his tailoring business simply ceased to exist, of course. His apprentices fled for their lives. Without men of our own, we could not go out in Taliban-ruled Afghanistan.

....

could tell knew what would happen
lintel top of the door
set off left
dwindled and dwindled became less and less

We depended on our neighbors and relatives for everything. We huddled in our house, eating what food they brought us when they could. Outside, widows like my mother were **cropping up in ever-greater numbers** in the streets to beg; and when the Taliban caught them, they beat them, because they were out without male escorts. We were wondering how **the end would come**. It had to come, it seemed.

....

cropping up in ever-greater numbers becoming more and more common

the end would come we were going to die

BEFORE YOU MOVE ON...

1. **Conclusions** Farah's father and sisters died when a rocket hit their house. Why could they not have a traditional burial?

2. **Summarize** How does Farah describe Afghanistan after the Taliban took control?

LOOK AHEAD What do Farah and her mother decide to do next? Read to page 131 to find out.

ESCAPE FROM
AFGHANISTAN

∞

One day we got a letter, hand-carried to us by some traveler. **Alas**, it was not from my brothers. It came from my mother's cousin in Quetta, a city on the Pakistan side of the Afghan border. We had **lost track of her** and did not even know she was there, but somehow, six months after my father's death, she had heard about the event and about our **quandary**.

Come to Quetta, she wrote. *Get across the border somehow, and then come directly to Quetta. Do not **tarry** in Peshawar. That is a Taliban stronghold, a Pashtun city. You won't be welcome there. In fact, you will be in danger, for the Taliban come from that region, and they are prejudiced against Hazaras. Peshawar is a dangerous place for two Hazara women on their own. Do not even go into the city, if you can avoid it. Just come to Quetta.* And she gave directions for

··

Alas Unfortunately
lost track of her not heard from her for a long time
quandary problem
tarry delay, wait

finding her house once we got to her city.

This cousin of my mother's had moved to Quetta some time ago. She had a settled life there. She had lost her husband, but she had a brother and two sons living in Turkmenistan. Those men had gotten out of Afghanistan during the Communist era. They had gone to Turkmenistan to study, and then, because the country had dissolved into civil war, they had simply stayed. They now worked in that former Soviet republic and sent bits of money from time to time; that's what my mother's cousin lived on.

Well, we talked it over with our neighbors and decided that we had to do it. We **made inquiries** and learned that we could pay a man to serve as our escort on the bus to Jalalabad. That would get us out of Taliban-dominated Kabul. From Jalalabad to the border, we would be on our own. As for getting across the border, no one knew what that entailed. And as for making the journey from the border to Quetta, that was like asking how to get from one part of the moon to another part. No one could give us any advice on that subject. We would just have to figure things out when we got there.

By the time we left Afghanistan, the warm days had come. We wrapped the few possessions we would take along in little cloth bundles. We could not take much, for we would have to carry whatever we took, and while I could not handle much of a load, my poor mother was in even worse shape. The day my father died, her asthma **took a turn for the worse**. Now she was rasping with every breath, and **exertion** of any kind

....

made inquiries asked questions
took a turn for the worse got worse than before
exertion activity

tightened up her air passages. We had no medicine for her condition. When it got bad, all she could do was rest, so the last thing we needed was extra baggage.

We made it to Jalalabad by bus. We could not have gotten there any other way. The stretch of road between Kabul and Jalalabad goes over some of the country's steepest mountains, cutting through two **rugged gorges**. The Kabul River pours through those gorges in a **series of thundering cataracts**, and the highway has been cut into nearly solid rock, folding back and forth, back and forth like a ribbon along the riverbank.

Once the road descended out of those gorges, the weather changed. The temperature rose. Now we were in the Jalalabad valley, which was dotted with groves of orange trees and lemon trees. The bus let us off in a crowded bazaar. We were frightened to be there alone and frightened to have to ask for advice and directions, but we addressed our questions to women as much as possible or to family groups that included women. In this way we found out how to get to the "other" bus station.

This other bus station wasn't really a station. There was no building, no ticket booth, and no station agent—nothing like that. The so-called bus station looked like any other part of the bazaar: It was just a road lined on both sides with merchants' stalls. Along this strip of bazaar, however, men cruised back and forth in vans they owned, looking for people who wanted to go to the border. If you just stood at the curb, they pulled over and offered you a ride.

Before we got on, though, other people waiting there for

....

tightened up her air passages made it hard to breathe
rugged gorges steep, narrow canyons
series of thundering cataracts group of very loud waterfalls

rides advised us to get some plastic bags. We didn't know why, but we figured we had better do whatever other travelers were doing. They **no doubt** knew more than we did. Curiously enough, some of the stalls in that vicinity sold plastic bags as if this were a normal travel need.

Shortly after we **took up our post** by the side of the road, a van pulled over. Instantly, a crowd surged toward its door. People fought and **threw elbows** to get to the front so they could board. That's how it was at the "bus station." Only the most aggressive travelers got rides. Each van could carry ten or twelve people, if they squeezed; and they always squeezed. The drivers wanted to make as much money as they could. We were unable to get onto the first van. We could not get on the next one, either. By the third one, however, I saw what we needed to do, and taking my mother by the arm, I shoved and pushed with the others until we made it to the door of the van.

It wasn't all that far from Jalalabad to the border, but we were traveling in the heat of mid-afternoon. Dust boiled up around the car and got in through the windows. My mother began to wheeze and gasp. I worried that she might stop breathing right then and there, so I tried to **shield** her with my body, tried to keep the other passengers from pressing in on her so that she would have her own space to breathe out of. Meanwhile, the dust mingled with the sweat running down my face, turning to mud by the time it reached my chin.

At that moment I discovered what the plastic bags were for: One of the men in the backseat vomited loudly, barely

....

no doubt probably
took up our post started standing
threw elbows pushed each other
shield protect, cover

getting his awful stew into his bag. The nasty odor immediately **pervaded** the entire van. **My nostrils puckered**, and I felt my own vomit rising. I grabbed for my bag. Within minutes, all of us passengers were filling up our plastic bags. No, it wasn't far from Jalalabad to the border, just a couple of hours, but that ride felt like it would never end.

About half a mile from the border the van pulled over to the side of the road. "This is as far as we go," the driver said. "That's the border up ahead. You see those two buildings and the gate between them? That's it. If you can get through that gate, you're in Pakistan. About half a mile up the road on the other side, if you can get to the other side, you'll find other cars like this one offering rides to Peshawar."

Well, we got out and started **trudging** toward the border station. We were not alone. The whole stretch of road was filled with people hoping to get across the border that day—hundreds of families. I don't know how many. I wasn't counting. I didn't count. I was distracted by the scene I saw up ahead.

The gate to Pakistan was closed, and I could see that the Pakistani border guards were letting no one through. People were pushing and shoving and jostling up against that gate, and the guards were driving them back. As we got closer, the crowd thickened, and I could hear the roar and clamor at the gate. The Afghans were yelling something, and the Pakistanis were yelling back. My mother was clutching her side and gasping for breath, trying to **keep up**. I felt desperate to get through, because the sun was setting, and if we got stuck here, what were

....

pervaded filled
My nostrils puckered It was hard to breathe
trudging walking slowly
keep up run with me

we going to do? Where would we stay? There was nothing here, no town, no hotel, no buildings, just the desert.

Yet we had no real chance of getting through. Big strong men were running up to the gate **in vain**. The guards had clubs, and they had **carbines**, too, which they turned around and used as weapons. Again and again, the crowd surged toward the gate and the guards drove them back with their sticks and clubs, swinging and beating until the crowd **receded**. And after that, for the next few minutes, on our side of the border, people milled about and muttered and stoked their own impatience and worked up their rage, until gradually the crowd gathered strength and surged against that gate again, only to be swept back.

We never even got close to the front. We got caught up in the thinning rear end of the crowd, and even so, we were part of each wave, pulled forward, driven back. It was hard for me to keep my footing, and my mother was clutching my arm now, just hanging on, just trying to stay close to me, because the worst thing would have been if we had gotten separated. Finally, I saw that it was no use. We were only risking injury. We drifted back, out of the crowd. In the thickening dusk we could hear the dull roar of people still trying to get past the border guards, but we receded into the desert, farther and farther back from the border gate.

Night was falling, and we were stranded out there in the open.

But at least it wasn't cold; that was a blessing. And at least we were not alone. For that, too, I felt grateful. Hundreds of us

....

in vain without success
carbines guns, rifles
receded moved back

were **hunkering** out there on the desert floor, in the shadows of the high hills that marked the border. We were clotted into family groups. Some groups managed to get fires going, which added a feeling of cheer. They chatted quietly around their fires, and we could hear their voices. There was something **companionable** about it, really. We were all just ordinary folks caught in a bad situation, sharing the same fate. No one there meant anybody harm.

Had I been alone, I would have felt frightened, but with that sea of families surrounding me, I felt safe, even if they were strangers. My mother and I had our little cloth bundles, in which we were each carrying some extra clothes, and we had our head scarves. We put those under our heads as pillows and slept under the stars. It wasn't bad. We did manage to catch some sleep.

Then dawn came, and we again had to make our way to the road and try to get across that border. What else could we do? We could not go back, nor could we stay in that wasteland indefinitely. We *had* to get through. But once again, the guards were keeping the gate closed, beating and hitting anyone who got close enough each time the crowd rushed.

On that second day, however, I learned that it was all a question of money. Someone told me about this, and then I watched closely and saw that it was true. Throughout the day, while some of the guards confronted the crowds, a few others lounged over to the side. People approached them quietly. **Money changed hands**, and the guards then let those people

....

hunkering camping and waiting
companionable friendly and social
Money changed hands They gave the guards money

quietly through a small door to the side. Hundreds could have flowed through the main gate had it been opened, but only one or two could get through the side door at a time. The fact that the guards were taking **bribes did us no good whatsoever**. We did not have the money to pay them. What little we had we would need to get from Peshawar to Quetta. And so the second day passed.

At the end of that day we found ourselves camping near a friendly family. We **struck up** a conversation with them. The woman told us that her husband, Ghulam Ali, had gone to look for another way across the border. He was checking out a goat path that supposedly went over the mountains several miles northeast of the border station. If one could get to Pakistan safely by that route, he would come back for his family. "You can go with us," the woman said.

Later that night her husband showed up. "It works," he said. "**Smugglers** use that path, and they bribe the guards to leave it unguarded. Of course, we don't want to run into any smugglers, either, but if we go late at night, we should be fine."

His wife then told him our story, and Ghulam Ali took pity on us. "Yes, of course you can come with us," he said. "But you have had two hard days. You will need some rest before you attempt this mountain crossing. Spend tonight here and sleep well, knowing that you will have nothing to do tomorrow except lounge around, rest, and catch your breath. Tomorrow, do not throw yourself against those border guards again. Let your only work be the gathering of your strength. Then

....

bribes did us no good whatsoever money to let people cross the border did not help us

struck up started

Smugglers Criminals, Thieves

tomorrow night we will all go over the mountain together, with God's grace. I will show you the way. If God wills it, we will follow that smugglers' path to safety. You and your mother are in my care now."

So we spent the whole next day there. It was terribly warm and we had no water, but we walked a little way and found a mosque that refugees like us had built over the years, so that people waiting to get across the border would have a place to say their prayers. We got some water to drink at the mosque, and we said *namaz* there, too. Somehow we obtained a bit of bread as well. I can't remember how **that turned up**, but there it was, and we ate it. **We sustained our strength.** After sunset we lay down just as if we were going to spend another night. In fact, I did fall asleep for a while. Long after dark—or early the next morning, to be exact, before the sun came up—that man shook us awake. "It's time," he said.

We got up and **performed our ablutions** quickly in the darkness, with just sand, because that's allowed when you have no access to water. We said our prayers. Then Ghulam Ali began to march into the darkness with his family, and we trudged along silently behind them. After several miles the path began to climb, and my mother began to wheeze. Her asthma was pretty bad at this point, poor thing. No doubt, her anxiety made it worse, but in such circumstances how could she rid herself of anxiety? It was no use knowing that her difficulty was rooted in anxiety, just as it was no use knowing that we could have moved more quickly if we had possessed wings.

....

that turned up we found bread

We sustained our strength. We rested so we would be strong.

performed our ablutions washed

Life is what it is. The path over that mountain was not actually very long, only a couple of miles. Steep as it was, we could have gotten over in little more than an hour if not for my mother. Because of her, we had to pause every few minutes, so our journey took many hours.

I myself hardly felt the exertion. I was walking quite well that day, quite athletically. I had that good prosthetic leg from Germany. The foot was a little worn by then, but not enough to slow me down. Thinking back, I'm puzzled, actually. How did I scale that mountain so easily? How did I climb down the other side? These days I find it hard to clamber up two or three flights of stairs, even. I don't know what made me so **supple** and strong that day, but I felt no hardship, no anxiety or fear, just concentration and intensity. Perhaps my mother's problems distracted me from my own. That might **account for it**. Perhaps desperation gave me energy and made me forget the rigor of the climb. Well, whatever the reason, I scrambled up like a goat. The family we were following had a girl only a bit younger than me, and she was moving slowly. Her family used my example to chide her. They kept saying, "Look at that girl. She's missing a leg, and yet she's going faster than you. Why can't you keep up? Hurry now!"

That Ghulam Ali was certainly a good man, so patient with us and so compassionate. He had never seen us before, and yet when he met us, he said, "I will help you." That's the thing about life. You never know when and where you will **encounter a spot of human decency**. I have felt alone in this world at

....

supple able, athletic

account for it be why

encounter a spot of human decency meet people who are kind

times; I have known long periods of being no one. But then, without warning, a person like Ghulam Ali just turns up and says, "I see you. I am on your side." Strangers have been kind to me when it mattered most. That sustains a person's hope and faith.

Anyway, climbing up that mountain on the Afghanistan side took some effort, but after we topped the crest, even my mother found the going down part fairly easy. We hardly stopped at all on the downward side. Going up took hours; coming down took minutes, or so it seemed.

As soon as we reached the bottom of the slope, Ghulam Ali told us we were now officially in Pakistan. We peered around. The landscape looked just the same here as it did back where we came from. And yet we were in Pakistan. We had escaped from Afghanistan. We started laughing. We couldn't stop. We tried to stop **our mouths with our palms**, and we could not do it. The laughter just **insisted on bursting forth from us**. Happiness filled our hearts. My mother's asthma disappeared **without a trace** for one whole hour. Yes, for one whole hour there, my mother could breathe. You might as well say we had been in prison for thirty years and had suddenly been released—that was the kind of joy we felt.

....

our mouths with our palms laughing by covering our mouths

insisted on bursting forth from us came out of our mouths

without a trace completely

BEFORE YOU MOVE ON...

1. **Summarize** Farah and her mother decided to go to Quetta in Pakistan. What were their plans? Reread pages 121–122.

2. **Conclusions** Reread pages 130–131. What did Farah learn about life after Ghulam Ali helped them?

LOOK AHEAD Read pages 132–142 to find out how Farah and her mother feel in Pakistan.

LIVING AS A REFUGEE

⌘

Finally, we forced our feet to move again. Just a few steps farther along we came to a cluster of little juice stands, businesses that had set up here to **cater** to smugglers. It was mid-morning by now and getting hot again. We bought some Cokes, some Fantas, and we drank it all and then laughed some more.

After that we hoisted our bundles and started walking. About a mile into Pakistan, just along the road there, we came to shops and hotels, restaurants and teahouses. We stopped at one of those places and **splurged** on a pot of milk tea, sweetened with honey and flavored with cardamom. It tasted delicious—**the flavor of delight itself**, I would say. And this little business district had sprung up to serve people crossing

....

cater sell

splurged spent more money than we should have

the flavor of delight itself it tasted great because we felt great

the border illegally. That's how many of us there were.

A cot happened to be sitting outside that teahouse, and we plopped down upon it and thought ourselves kings and queens. Yes, the exhilaration of that moment made us feel like royalty. *Allah*, our hearts were saying, *we surrender to you, body and soul! Accept us, Lord!* Such was the joy we felt.

It's true that my mother and I had no idea where we were going to spend the night at that point. We did not know where our next meal would come from, who might harm us in the sinister city of Peshawar, or how we would get to Quetta. Actually, we did not know one single thing about our future, except that the road ahead of us brimmed with difficulty, danger, and darkness. In any other circumstance we would have been trembling with anxiety. Yet, in the midst of this terrible time, we **exuded exuberance**. And why? Because we had reached *this spot*. The future lay in God's hands, but we had reached *this spot*. It's a good thing that a person can pause at times and take pleasure in difficulties overcome, because if we had spared one droplet of thought on our future, that thought would have stripped us of joy and drenched us with dread. Instead, for a moment there, one memorable moment, we **tasted unmitigated happiness**.

Well, once we had finished our milk tea and rested our bones and sunk back to Earth, Ghulam Ali, that same poor fellow, said. "What are your plans? If you have no place to stay, come with us. I have a friend in Peshawar. That's where we are going until we **get our bearings**. He will be glad to welcome you as well."

....

exuded exuberance were very excited

tasted unmitigated happiness felt completely happy

get our bearings decide where to go next

I said, "We don't want to stay in Peshawar. We have been told it is dangerous there for Hazaras. We want to go to Quetta. How can we get there from here? Do you know?"

"Never mind about Quetta right now," Ghulam Ali told us. "This friend of mine is almost like family. Come to his place with us for the night. The morning will be soon enough to talk about Quetta. If you insist, I'll get you a train ticket in the morning."

So we all boarded a bus for Peshawar. The road turned and twisted through an immense notch in the mountains. That bus smelled awful, and when we got to the city, that smelled, too. Peshawar was full of open sewers and cars, and the air was so polluted, we felt like we were smoking every time we took a breath. Ghulam Ali introduced us to his friend, himself a poor man with a large family of his own. And now this man was taking in Ghulam Ali and his family, and then to have us **drop in on top of it all**—we were too much. We two were **extra beyond extra**. It just wouldn't do. They could not keep us. We saw that for ourselves, no one had to say a thing. We stayed with that family for a single night, but even in that short time we made the house too intolerably crowded. We would have moved on even if we had not considered Peshawar so dangerous.

So the next day we gave Ghulam Ali all the money we had left from the sale of my mother's jewelry. It was Afghan currency. Ghulam Ali took it to **the black market**, turned it into Pakistani **rupees**, bought us two train tickets to Quetta, and brought back the change.

....

drop in on top of it all arrive unexpectedly, too
extra beyond extra much more than they could support
the black market the illegal traders of goods
rupees money

We boarded the train around twilight and spent the next two nights and days riding to Quetta. It took that long not just because Quetta is quite far from Peshawar, but also because the train went slowly, and it stopped every few minutes, always with **a great deal of clanking and hissing**. The weather was steamingly hot the whole way, very hot. And the train was crowded, mostly with men.

In Afghanistan we were accustomed to sitting in a corner and **keeping ourselves inconspicuous** when men were around. To be among male strangers on that train was very hard. We wrapped ourselves as tightly as we could manage in all the veils and scarves we possessed and kept as quiet as we could. I'm not sure anyone could have known if we were even human, much less whether we were men or women. A casual observer might just as easily have mistaken us for giant cocoons or creatures of a kind unknown to science.

Were there any other women on the train? A few, but they were traveling with their families. They all had men to protect them. We were the only women traveling on our own. The journey to Quetta felt two years long.

The men on that train all looked similar to me. It must have been the way men looked in this region. They had swarthy skin, wiry frames, **kohl-rimmed eyes**, and thick lips. They all wore big bushy beards. I could not help but fear them because they all looked like Taliban. Each one might have been a perfectly decent man if you got to know him, but we could not doubt that we had come to the **very mother soil** of the Taliban,

....

a great deal of clanking and hissing a lot of noise
keeping ourselves inconspicuous trying not to be noticed
kohl-rimmed eyes blackened eyelids
very mother soil central area; base

the place where such men were grown. Time **passed hard** among such men. I slept a little, but my mother never really slept at all, especially at night. She stayed alert out of concern for me, standing guard to make sure that no one tried to take me away from her.

No one bothered us, however. No one even spoke to us, except occasional vendors who only wanted to sell us something: mango juice, apple juice, and I don't remember what else. I don't remember anyone vending food. In any case, we didn't buy anything. We had brought some water on board with us, and we had a bag of bread, which Ghulam Ali's friend in Peshawar had given us. What we didn't have was money, or at least **none to spare**. I think we had the equivalent of about one hundred dollars on us, total. But we were nervous about spending any of it, in part because we didn't know what **catastrophes were coming up**: We had to save our money for unknown emergencies. But also, we didn't want anyone to see us spending money. If anyone knew we had cash on us, they might try to rob us, we thought. For two days and two nights, therefore, we huddled in a corner and just tried to look inconspicuous.

When we got to Quetta, we dared to take a cab to my mother's cousin's address; we were so close to refuge now, we could afford to spend a little. The only problem was, we didn't know what a cab should cost. An Afghan widow and her ten-year-old daughter—how could we know about such things? When we told the cabdriver where we were going, he said the ride would cost seventy rupees. We didn't know if that was high or low, but we protested his price on principle so that he would not think he had **gotten hold of some country bumpkins whom he could just exploit**. Oh, we hectored and negotiated valiantly until at last we bargained him down to fifty rupees! We felt so proud of ourselves, so worldly.

Later we found out that the standard fare for that distance was twenty rupees.

Peshawar was dangerous for us because so many Pashtuns live there. Lots of Pashtuns live in Quetta, too, but one part of Quetta has a lot of immigrants from the Bamiyan valley, the heartland of the Hazara people's territory in Afghanistan. They came to Quetta long before Pakistan even existed as a separate country. They gained Pakistani citizenship at the moment of the country's birth. By this time they had deep roots in the city. Many of them have nice houses, big yards—all that stuff. The Hazara district in Quetta is called Mariabad. These former Afghan Hazaras speak a language all their own, a mixture of Farsi and Urdu, with a **smattering of English stirred into the mix**.

During our one night in Peshawar, we asked everyone we met about my brothers: Had they seen anyone who fit that description? No one had any information. Everywhere we went in Quetta, we posed the same questions and got no answers. Eventually, the women who lived next door to us in Kabul got out of the country and settled in Peshawar. They, too, made inquiries all along the way and all around the town about their boys and ours, trying to find out what happened to them,

....

gotten hold of some country bumpkins whom he could just exploit met some simple people whom he could cheat

smattering of English stirred into the mix small amount of English, too

desperate to know if they at least made it out of the country alive; but they got no answers either.

Before we left Peshawar, we had described my brothers to Ghulam Ali and begged him to keep an eye out for them. We got Ghulam Ali's address and wrote to him from my mother's cousin's house, so that if he ever chanced to meet my brothers, he could tell them where to find us. We gave him a phone number. "Tell them to call us," we said hopefully. But we never got that phone call. We tried to stay hopeful, but it wasn't easy. We weren't getting any **breaks to keep hope alive**.

In Quetta we moved in with my mother's cousin, but this was another poor family with a tiny house, and we made this place too crowded as well. The money they received from Turkmenistan **sufficed only for their own needs**. They got nothing extra just because we had arrived. After a year or so the situation became **intolerable**.

Finally I said, "Well, we will go and rent a room of our own."

But at first no one would rent to us. "You are two women alone," they said. "We can't rent to you unless you have a man with you." What were people in our situation supposed to do? Eventually, we did find a room, however. A family with a big house agreed to rent us one small room for half price on the condition that we would babysit for them, clean their house, and do other odd jobs as needed.

This arrangement worked for a while, but it could not last, for even though I was taking in a little sewing, making practical use at last of the skills I had learned from my father,

....

breaks to keep hope alive news that would make us feel better

sufficed only for their own needs was enough only for their own family

intolerable terrible, impossible

the money I earned paid only for food—and for the **bills we incurred** each time I had to get my mother to a hospital, which was often. We eventually ran out of money, which meant we couldn't pay even the reduced rent, so the family we were living with **evicted us**. At this point we had to leave the city and **throw ourselves on the mercy of** the United Nations. We ended up in a big refugee camp that had been set up just outside Quetta.

The camp was just an immense collection of tents out in the open. My mother and I got one tent to ourselves. When winter came on, the temperature dropped and the wind began to howl. Sitting in our tent, wrapped in a thin blanket, I watched my mother lose weight and color. Her cough grew worse.

One morning she began to suck in breath as if she were breathing through a pillow, working every muscle in her skinny body just to draw in enough air to go on living. Believe me, this sight terrified me. And what could I do? We were miles out of town. No doctor would come out here. I had to get her to a hospital.

Somehow I got her to walk with me, leaning on my shoulder, staggering and coughing, to the road that ran through the middle of the camp. Here, people could flag down one of these little three-wheeled vehicles that ran people to town and back. These jitneys were like modified motorcycles with a driver in front and two seats behind him, facing backward.

The hospital was crowded, but my mother was admitted. Every patient in that hospital had a crowd of family members

....

bills we incurred debts we had to pay
evicted us made us leave
throw ourselves on the mercy of ask for help from

milling about their bed. Families ate there, cooking their meals on gas burners at the patient's bedside, and some slept there on the floor. The conditions were not exactly what you would call **sanitary**.

They put my mother in a bed next to a girl who was dying of some illness. The poor girl lay there, gasping for breath and wincing with pain, while her family sat around her, telling stories, eating nuts, cooking lentils. The thing is, she took a long time to die. The family had been there so long, they had gotten quite used to the girl's gasping and groaning. They didn't hear it anymore. They had spent all their tears and used up all the comfort they had to give. Now they were tired of the hospital and the girl's illness, so they had gone back to their normal routines, even though they were **eking out these routines** in the presence of their dying child. Everything becomes normal if it just keeps going long enough.

When the girl finally did die, no one witnessed it except me. I happened to be looking at her at that moment. I saw her stiffen up and jerk a few times, and then she was gone. Her family didn't notice, but then a moment later they looked over and said, "Oh." This is how it was in the hospital to which I had brought my mother.

I wondered if I would someday stop hearing my mother's rasping breath even as it sounded in my ears, if I would grow so **inured to** her suffering. It had not happened yet. Every time she flinched or winced, a spasm jolted through my body, too.

On this occasion my mother's breathing eased eventually.

....

sanitary clean

eking out these routines doing these daily chores with difficulty

inured to used to

I don't know if the doctors did anything in particular to help her. She may have recovered just from being indoors, out of the cold, and sheltered from the wind. Once she felt better, however, we were discharged from the hospital. They would not let us stay. They needed the bed.

So we went back to our tent in the refugee camp. **From time to time**, I took a jitney into town to look for sewing work. My mother stayed home, if you can call a tent a home. We ate the plain, dull food the aid organizations distributed in the refugee camp. The **pittance** I made from sewing covered just the hospital bills each time my mother had an asthma attack. Into the hospital, back to the tent; into the hospital, back to the tent—that became the rhythm of our life.

Unfortunately, I can't say that rhythm was never-changing. For once we started heading into another winter, my mother's overall health declined. The best days came along more rarely. On her worst days she sometimes **hit new lows. My own spirits kept sinking, too.** I had no source of hope out of which to nourish my struggle. When you see some possibility of getting out of a pit, you can draw strength from the idea of where you will be once you get out: You see a goal worth fighting for. If the best you can hope for is to sink more slowly, struggle comes to feel pointless. You say to yourself, *If I'm going to sink anyway, what does it matter whether I sink quickly or slowly?* You lose your drive.

I was coming to this point. Finally, one day, when my mother had another attack, when I struggled once again to

....

From time to time Sometimes, Occasionally

pittance small amount of money

hit new lows was sicker than ever before

My own spirits kept sinking, too. I felt hopeless, too.

help her to the side of the road to flag down one more jitney, it struck me that she was not going to make it through another winter in this refugee camp. If we didn't get back to the city, my mother would be dead by spring.

Fortunately, my mother survived that attack, but as soon as I got her back to the tent, I went to town to look for a place to live. I obviously had no prospect of finding what you might call a real job, a means of supporting us in decent comfort. No one was going to hire a one-legged twelve-year-old Afghan girl in Quetta. At last, however, I found a way to move back to the city to a warm place, sheltered from the **elements**. I found a family that would give us free room and board in exchange for work. So, in the winter of 2000, my mother and I left the UN refugee camp and moved into a tiny room little bigger than a closet, the two of us together.

I was still sewing, making just enough to pay for medicine and hospital visits for my mom. My mother's cousin could still spare us a bit of money once in a while. We could buy our own food sometimes—but we had nothing left over. Once I got my mother and me into this situation **with the room and board in exchange for work**, there was no way I could get us out of it again. Essentially, we became slaves.

....

elements bad weather

with the room and board in exchange for work where I worked and was paid with a place to live

BEFORE YOU MOVE ON...

1. **Conclusions** Reread pages 132–133. Farah and her mother felt happy when they reached Pakistan. Why?

2. **Cause and Effect** Reread pages 141–142. What caused Farah to decide to leave the refugee camp?

LOOK AHEAD Read pages 143–152 to find out how Farah feels about her life story.

TALKING TO GOD

The room we rented was in the house of a **fairly well-to-do merchant family**. When they said we could have free room and board in exchange for work, they really meant work.

It started at dawn, when the mullah chanted the *aazan*, the morning call to prayer. They had five children in this household, and the little ones started crying right then. At that point I had to get up and start taking care of the children so that everyone else could sleep.

The yard here was paved, it was all cement, and every day I had to scrub it spotlessly clean on my hands and knees, with a brush and a pail of soapy water. Then I had to rinse it down. My prosthesis started to wear out from getting wet and then from my dragging it across the rough cement. The mother in this household **squared away her domestic affairs** by midmorning and then went out. I don't know where. She left her

---

fairly well-to-do merchant family family that owned a store and had a lot of money

squared away her domestic affairs did her work in the house

children for me to watch. And those kids were oh so unruly, so naughty. There was nothing I could do with them; I didn't know how to control them. I was only thirteen or so myself. If I so much as spoke a harsh word to them, much less scolded them, they complained to their mother when she came home, and then I got scolded or punished or deprived of food.

The oldest of the five children in this family was a girl just about my age or a little younger. She was bigger than me, because I am so short, but she was no older. That girl **harassed me endlessly.** She took great delight in bossing me around. I couldn't stand for someone my own age to lord it over me, giving me orders just to watch me obey. I hated taking those orders, but I did everything she asked, though I had difficulty **holding my tongue.**

That girl found a thousand ways to **choke the spirit out of me.** Sometimes she saw me busy with a job her mother had given me and she ordered me to leave that job and do some piece of work for her. She put me in positions where I either had to disobey her or leave her mother's job undone. Either way, I would get in trouble.

She always followed me around as I scrubbed the yard, saying, "You missed a spot, get back here. You missed this spot." Then when I had scrubbed that spot again and moved on, she would say, "No! That wasn't good enough! Get back here!"

When I finished a chore, she would come over and stare at me, until I had to ask, "What else should I do?" She would **hem and haw** and finally think of something, then watch me as

---

harassed me endlessly was always mean to me
holding my tongue being quiet
choke the spirit out of me make me sad
hem and haw try to decide

I worked. She never did any work herself, and I wanted to shout, *All right, I'll do your job, but what are you staring at me for? Go away!*

Of course we both knew why she was watching me like that: She was waiting for me to make a mistake, a chance for her to say, "Aha! You wretch, start over! Do it again!"

When she got tired of **chastising** me, she would go to the living room and turn on the television. After I finished every job assigned to me, every last possible piece of work I could imagine around the house, I would go and watch television, too, from the back of the room. But as soon as this girl **noticed my presence**, she would turn the television off, so that I would go away. And then as soon as I left, I would hear her turn that TV on again.

Sometimes her mother would cook something for us, but the girl always insisted on bringing it to us herself. "Don't bother with that, A'ika," she would say. "I'll take it to them." *A'ika* is the word for "mom" in the **dialect** these people spoke.

Well, she would bring the food to our little room and dish out a little for us and throw the rest away. When her mother said, "Did you give them their food?" this girl would say, "Oh, yes, A'ika, I gave them plenty, and they sure **gobbled it up**." I, of course, had to keep my mouth shut and contain my angry thoughts. It seems hard to imagine, but if I had complained, it would have made things even worse.

Sometimes her mother would sit the two of us down and say, "Okay, girls, here are all these clothes. I want you to iron

---

chastising being mean to
noticed my presence realized I was there
dialect language
gobbled it up ate it quickly

them together." She acted like we were companions and that this would be a fun thing for us to do as a team. But as soon as the mother left, that girl would go watch television. Then, just before her mother was due home, she'd come back and pretend she had been working all along. When her mother entered the room, she would launch into loud complaints about my laziness, about how I had not helped her, how she had been forced to do all this ironing by herself, and then her mother would warn me to improve my behavior if I wanted to **stay on the premises**. It made me **indignant**, but there was nothing I could do about it.

I don't know what motivated this girl. For my mother's sake, I never said one complaining word to her or about her. My mother was sick, and if we got kicked out of this place, I didn't know where I could take her. My mother knew what was going on, though. She knew how this girl was ordering me around, **slandering me**, and casting blame on me for the things she herself had done wrong; but my mother kept telling me, "Bear up. Let it go, Daughter. Do as she tells you. Don't let it bother you."

And so because of my mother, I tolerated my situation. Much later, here in America, my friend Alyce showed us a tape one night, a movie called *Cinderella*. In the middle of the tape I started to cry. I thought I was crying for Cinderella, but looking back, I realize that I saw my own story in hers. That's why *Cinderella* affected me so sharply.

I grew tired of life itself in that house. My prosthetic leg was wearing out. The foot had cracked, and I could hardly walk on

....

stay on the premises continue living there
indignant very angry
slandering me saying untrue, bad things about me

it anymore. Someone told my mother of a place in Quetta that made prosthetic limbs, so we went there one day. They had only ready-made prosthetics made of wood instead of plastic like mine. Wooden prosthetics are very heavy, and this shop had only big ones, made for men, large men.

The worker there said he could saw the foot off one of these large legs and glue it to the end of my prosthetic. I had no choice but to accept this solution, so I said yes.

The foot he gave me was about one and half times the size of my real foot. It was a great big heavy thing, too. He glued this man-size foot onto my girl's prosthetic, and my mother and I headed home in a **rickshaw**.

Near the house we got out of the rickshaw and started to walk the final block. Suddenly, the foot fell off. I tripped and fell, right there in the street. My mother panicked. "Stay there," she shouted—as if could go anywhere without my leg—and she ran to get us another rickshaw so we could return to the prosthetics shop. In her **frantic haste**, however, she left me just lying in the street.

I looked up—a bus was coming. The driver didn't slow down. He assumed I was an able-bodied person who could get out of the way if I wanted to. I think he assumed I was lying there **to give him needless trouble**. I was trying to stand up, but I wasn't used to doing so with a footless prosthetic. I fell over again and had to drag myself out of the way on my knees, pushing and pulling myself with my hands. The bus driver slowed down to curse me for making him slow down and then

---

rickshaw cart pulled by a person

frantic haste frightened rush

to give him needless trouble to make him frustrated and angry

sped off. In the meantime, neighborhood children clustered around me, chattering. I felt humiliated.

My mother came back with another rickshaw, and we returned to the prosthetics shop. The man admitted he had done a poor job, and he set about gluing the foot to my prosthetic more securely. As far as that went, he did a good job. I had a foot from then on, but it was heavy and ungainly and much larger than my other foot. Still, I had to **make do**, for it was better than no foot at all.

My mother's asthma, meanwhile, kept getting worse. And with that girl constantly lording it over me, **the whole world seemed to press down on my shoulders**. Some days I thought I could not bear it. I thought, *Oh, this weight! This weight is too heavy for me. This weight!*

And all this time I brooded. In my heart I kept asking why all this was happening to me. When I came home from Germany and saw the pitiful state of Afghanistan, when I saw my people making war on one another every day, when I lost my family to the ravages of that war, I grew angry with God. Yes, angry with him. Why should I deny this? It's the truth.

If God is there, I reasoned, *if God is so nice, like they say—if God is so powerful—if he can really do anything in the world, why is he doing* this? In the Koran, you know, it says that God is compassionate and all-forgiving. It says that God wants only the best for humanity. But how could I believe it? In fact, I was too distressed to pay much attention to believing in God. I was too beaten down by my hardships to worship him.

....

make do use it

the whole world seemed to press down on my shoulders
I felt that everything was against me

Then one night, one certain night, something happened. I wish I knew the date. For my own satisfaction, I wish I knew, but I was not paying attention to the calendar since one day felt so much like the next. I just know that one night, after the rest of the family had gone to bed, I went outside onto that cement yard, which was still moist from the scrubbing I had given it that day. My problems were **boiling in my heart**—my ailing mother, my hurting legs, my eroding prosthetic. . . . This girl who endlessly tormented me had gone to bed, but her voice kept **shrilling away** in my head, shouting orders. All these things buzzed inside me like hornets released from a hive. I looked up at the stars, those same stars I had gazed upon with so much wonder when I was in second grade. And then—somehow—that long-forgotten sense of wonder came upon me again. I felt myself drawn up into all that space.

I surrendered my will. I just let it happen.

With my face turned up to the night sky, I spoke directly to God, spoke to him from my heart. I said, *Enough. Oh, my dear God. Get me out of this. God-darling, forgive me. I can't hold up all this weight by myself anymore. Please! I'll hold up most of it, but you hold up some of it. Whatever I've done wrong in the past, I can't change that now. Between you and me, let's say that what's done is done. All I can do now about the past is ask you to forgive me. I plead with you. All I can do is promise to be good, to remember you from now on always. I* **relinquish** *all of myself to you—no more resistance. Oh, please, God, help me. I can't hold up this weight anymore.*

That's what I said in my heart. In fact, that's what I *screamed,*

....

boiling in my heart making me feel bad
shrilling away screaming, shrieking
relinquish give

but not out loud. I spoke it just in my heart, only in my heart. I didn't make a sound. I was alone, but if anybody had been watching me at that moment, they would have seen nothing but that same **little mouse of a Farah** as always, standing quietly in the yard. Nonetheless, something was happening, something big. For the first time, truly and totally, I was surrendering to Allah.

And with that surrender, a change began. I felt it in that moment. I felt it ever increasingly in the days that followed. What was this change? My attention turned toward God. And the more I attended to God, the more I discovered how to be patient and tolerant and how to relax. When that girl snapped her orders at me, I let it wash away, I let it go, I absorbed none of her spite and hatred, and so she failed to plant any seeds of bitterness inside me. **Negativity stopped sprouting in my heart.** I grew so calm, so serene that even the girl who was bossing me around noticed the change and eased up on me.

After that, every day and every night, I said *namaz* at all the prescribed times. When the mullah chanted the *aazan* in the morning, I got up and washed myself and said a full set of prayers before anyone else in the household woke up. Throughout the day, when the call to prayer sounded, I stopped whatever I was doing, found a quiet spot, and turned my face to Mecca. No one dared tell me to stop performing the holy rituals and go back to doing household errands. Strangely enough, whenever I was absorbed in solitary prayer, I felt I had company. I felt *somebody's* presence and tenderness embracing me.

....

little mouse of a Farah quiet person I was

Negativity stopped sprouting in my heart. I did not hate her anymore.

I began to perform more than the five required prayers. Late at night I went out at the darkest hour, two or three a.m., with my Precious-Koran in hand. I performed *namaz*, and then afterward, looking up at the stars, I talked to God. So many stars were shining up there in the darkness—shining down on me! I remembered the wonderful things my second-grade teacher had told me, about the sky being so large and the stars being bigger than Earth and looking small only because they were so inconceivably far away, and in those moments the **grandeur of the universe exalted me** and I felt the power of God.

And yet I felt his nearness, too, and I had no trouble confessing my troubles to him as **intimately** as I might to a loving friend. I silently said, *Allah-dear, my mother is suffering so! When will she be released from her hardships?* I said, *God-dear, this leg of mine is wearing away. When it's gone, what will I do? Without my leg, I'm hardly even a person. I can't even get my own self to the bathroom. When my prosthetic is gone, what I am I going to do?*

No sooner had I posed such questions in my heart than I felt a warmth glowing and growing from the middle of me, and I knew that God was listening to me, that God was nearby, very close indeed, an invisible light, a bodiless friend, a smiling power. I had such a strong and positive feeling about God being there.

One night, looking up at the heavens, I saw a single star **detach itself from the light-studded dome** and streak across the night sky.

....

grandeur of the universe exalted me beauty of space excited me

intimately closely

detach itself from the light-studded dome fall away from the other stars

Then it was gone, but I knew that star meant something.

And indeed, a few days later, I woke up one morning to hear the news. A thousand Afghan refugees were to be rescued from Pakistan and taken to America!

My heart spoke again. *This comes from God*, it said. *My mother and I will be **among the thousand**. Thank you, God.* I knew that in his compassion Allah had decided to save me from this place. And that made me feel so calm and wonderful.

....

My heart spoke again. My heart felt hopeful again.

among the thousand *one of the thousand of people to go to America*

BEFORE YOU MOVE ON...

1. **Paraphrase** Reread page 146. What did Farah mean when she wrote that she saw her own story in *Cinderella*?

2. **Mood** Reread pages 149–152. Describe the mood of the chapter after Farah writes of her surrender to God.

LOOK AHEAD Read to page 169 to find out if Farah convinces her mother to go to America.

Making the List

No one knew who was going to take all these refugees to
America, and most of us Afghans didn't really think about it.
I guess we assumed that the American government was going
to do this thing. We were wrong about that, actually: It was
a private Christian organization called World Relief, but I
learned this only later. At the time I didn't care about such
details. I just wanted to know how to **sign up**.

I confess I never saw the announcement with my own
eyes. People said it was on television, on the radio, and in the
newspapers, but I never saw it or heard it or read it—I couldn't
read. I **picked up** the news from other people. Many others
probably learned about it the same way—from rumor. **Like a
coup d'etat**, it was suddenly the topic of every conversation

....

sign up apply
picked up heard
Like a coup d'etat Like the sudden overthrow of a
government

one morning. The whole neighborhood was talking about it. I **kept my ears open**, and that's how I learned that they were especially interested in taking widows and orphans. That's how you qualified to go.

After that, up and down our street, as soon as the mullah chanted the *aazan* for morning prayers, you heard compound doors banging open as groups of women, with their children, left to make their way to the nearest bus stop.

At first, according to the rumors, you had to apply at an office in a **posh** neighborhood within the city. That was where the Americans had their operation. But so many people came to apply that the Americans could not even open their doors the first day. They looked out and saw the whole street jammed with women and children as far as the eye could see. When they tried to let in just one, the whole crowd tried to get in. The workers inside the office panicked and put their shoulders to the door to squeeze it shut against the mob. Outside, the pushing and shoving **graduated to** punching and pulling of hair. Women and children and the few men who happened to be there all began to **raise such a commotion** that the police had to come. A lot of wealthy property owners lived in that neighborhood, rich Pakistanis with marble-tiled houses and fragrant gardens. They didn't want crowds of Afghan refugees clamoring and fighting in their leafy lanes. They told the Americans to process the refugees somewhere else. We learned all this from the buzz—the rumors and the gossip.

In any case, the Americans moved their operation to a place

---

kept my ears open listened carefully

posh fancy, wealthy

graduated to became

raise such a commotion be so violent

outside the city. No bus went to that location, and you couldn't get there by walking. It was too far away. If you wanted to apply for the program, you had to get to this special place by car. Most of the refugee widows didn't have cars, but even so, every morning, you heard them leaving their compounds in droves. They were hiring jitneys to take them out of town.

Right from the start, I announced that I was going to apply. The family we were living with told us to forget it. Some of the other Afghan refugees we knew in the neighborhood also **scoffed at** my determination. "Why would they pick you, of all people?" they said initially.

And I said, "Why not me? Why not my mother? She's a widow. I am an orphan: We qualify if anyone does."

And then they said, "How can you even think of dragging your poor sick mother off to America? Inconsiderate girl! Don't you know how far it is to America? Your mother will probably die in the airplane going over, may God not will it, and then where will you be?"

"Where am I now," I said, "that I should cling to this place?"

My mother, however, took what all these people were saying **to heart**. "My child, my child," she fretted, "what have folks like us to do with America? I'm too sick to travel. I don't want to die on an airplane. Don't make me go to America to die among strangers. I don't want to be buried in their soil."

I tried to tell her, "Mama, America is like Germany. I've been to Germany, and I know what it's like there. It's a good place, trust me. You will **recover your health** there. They have

....

scoffed at joked about
to heart as the truth
recover your health get better

good doctors, and the state will help. Don't be afraid. It's better for you if we go. You will finally find some **respite** from all the hardships you have endured."

But my frightened mother only wept. "It's too late for me," she lamented. She could barely get the words out through her coughing. "I don't have long to live. I don't want to turn to dust in foreign soil. Let me pass from the world here, where at least I know people. Let me be buried in this soil—that's all I ask."

Then I **lost my composure**. "What about me?" I shouted. "If you die, what will become of me, Mama? Who will protect me if something should happen to you? Whose house should I live in? A single girl can't live by herself in the cities of Pakistan or Afghanistan! Are you waiting for someone to marry me? Do you think that's how I will be saved, Mama? Forget it! No one is going to marry me! Here in Pakistan, if a girl **has so much as a mole to mar her beauty, she gets no suitors**! And you *know* that! If her face is not pale enough, if her eyebrows are too thick, if she falls short of physical perfection in any way . . . and I'm missing a *leg*, Mama! Who will take me? In America it's different. There, if I'm alone, I can survive, I can live. No one will look down on me for being single. No one will attack me—the law won't allow it. There, I can go to school, learn something, build a future for myself. Here? If a girl lives alone in Pakistan, it's a defect, a disgrace. They will never let me live my life here. Nor am I healthy, you know! I can't go out and labor for my bread. We *have* to do this. I don't care what anyone says! I *will* do it. In your name and mine, I will go apply."

---

respite rest

lost my composure got angry

has so much as a mole to mar her beauty, she gets no suitors is not beautiful, no one will marry her

In this way I tried to sway my mother, but then these people we were living with scared her with even stronger warnings, stories they **picked up from the rumor mill**. "This whole thing is a trick," they said. "Think about it. Why would anyone take a thousand widows to America? Think about it, you fools! Why only widows? Isn't it obvious? *Because widows have no men to protect them.* Widows and orphans are easy prey. Don't you know how much it costs to take a person to America? Have you ever heard of anyone getting something for nothing in this world? These people have **motives**. They're going to sell Farah into slavery in America. Everybody knows what's really going on. Rich Americans have already placed their orders: They want so many widows, so many orphans. Wait and see. The orphans will be sold as slaves, and the widows, the older ones, will be taken directly to a soap factory. *Because that's what they do with old women in America.* Haven't you heard? They make soap out of them!"

That's what people were saying in Pakistan. **Self-proclaimed experts lectured and hectored** my mother. They had read it somewhere, they had seen it somewhere, they had heard it from a real authority: Americans made old women into soap! My mother trembled at such tales. She believed them. "My child, my child, people know what they're talking about," she pleaded with me. "Have compassion for your poor mother. Don't take me to America, to this awful fate!"

Every day we argued and we both cried. I couldn't back down. I just wouldn't. I had seen a star fall from the sky. I knew

---

picked up from the rumor mill heard from other people

motives reasons for doing what they do

Self-proclaimed experts lectured and hectored People who thought they knew everything told

this opportunity was meant for me. Sometimes I pleaded with my mother on my knees, clutching at her skirts. Sometimes I just sat and reasoned with her. I described all the things I had seen in Germany, patiently, again and again. I told her not to listen to people in this neighborhood, they were ignorant. They didn't know.

And at first, of course, I alarmed my mother with words like these—I, a mere girl, was calling adult men ignorant! I, a **nonliterate thirteen-year-old child**, was challenging the wisdom of people much older than myself, some of whom could read. But I kept arguing from **the authority of my experience, I clung to that**. I had *been* to Germany. I had *seen* that world with my own eyes. It wasn't like they said.

At last I wore down my mother's resistance. She said, "Okay, we'll apply for this. But I'll do it. You stay home. There is no need for you to go."

I said, "No, Mama. You stay home. If you go, you'll have an asthma attack when the shoving and pushing starts, and what will you do then?"

But my mother countered, saying, "No, Farah. If *you* go, when the pushing and shoving starts, your leg will fall off, and what will *you* do then?"

So we **bickered** this way, back and forth, her asthma against my prosthetic, until we finally came to a compromise. We would both go, the two of us together.

I sought out a woman named Zaybah, who was organizing rides in our neighborhood. "Zaybah" means "beautiful," and

....

nonliterate thirteen-year-old child young girl who could not read or write

the authority of my experience, I clung to that what I knew to be true and would not forget it

bickered argued

the name suited this woman, for she certainly did a beautiful thing for all of us. Zaybah knew a man who owned a Suzuki—something like a cross between a rickshaw and a real car. For a **set fee**, this man was willing to take passengers out to the application station in the morning and bring them back at the end of the day. Zaybah paid him his fee each night and then lined up riders to share the cost. She told people where to meet and what time the ride was leaving. The more riders she signed up, the less each rider had to pay.

I put my mother and me on Zaybah's list. The next morning, a little before the **appointed time**, we went out and stood by the side of the road with the other hopeful passengers. We were all women, because people were saying that only widows should bother applying, widows and their children. Some of the women waiting with us that morning confessed that they did not know if they were widows. Their husbands had disappeared, but whether they had been killed or hauled off to a Taliban prison, they didn't know. They had, however, decided to try to go to America, although the possibility that they were abandoning their husbands filled them with doubt and anguish.

The mullah had just finished chanting his call to morning prayer. The sun had not yet come up. The Suzuki came along in the dark and pulled up to the curb. This small vehicle is open in the front, where the driver sits, but it has a **canopy** over the back. The passengers sit behind the driver on two benches that face each other, one along this side, one along that. It seats six

....

set fee price that never changed
appointed time time we had to be there
canopy covering for shade; top

comfortably, but eight can squeeze in. This morning, however, Zaybah had signed up twelve riders. As I said, she always signed up as many as she could, in order to reduce the cost per person. We crammed into the seats, we sat on the floor between the seats, we hung on to the outside—anything to get to the place where applications were being taken.

The man drove us through the quiet darkness of Quetta. About half an hour after leaving the **city limits**, we came to an isolated compound in the middle of an open field. In Pakistan, when people develop a property, they start by enclosing an area with high walls. After that, when they get to it, they **erect structures** inside the walls. Here, we saw no evidence of buildings inside the yard. No rooftops poked above the walls. And there was nothing else in that **vicinity**—no buildings, no other compounds—just this **featureless road running on to** some unknown destination, and the open fields, and this mud enclosure.

We arrived at about five o'clock in the morning in order to be first in line, but we were too late. Others had gotten up even earlier. Hundreds of people already stood waiting outside the gate of that compound. We had no choice but to take up our positions behind them all. Slowly, the hours passed, and as darkness gave way to daylight, more and more people arrived, until at last many thousands of us stood waiting for that gate to open.

As the sun rose, so did the temperature. Quetta gets quite hot in the summer, way above one hundred degrees on normal

....

city limits city
erect structures build buildings
vicinity surrounding area
featureless road running on to plain road going to

days. We had no water, and there was nowhere to get any here in this desolate wasteland. But then, as the morning went along, vendors began to arrive, for wherever great crowds gather, vendors see opportunities to make money. An instant bazaar took shape along that road—people selling food, selling water, selling fruit juice, selling ice cream. But we had no money to spare, and besides, we did not want to lose our place in line, for even though hundreds of people had arrived ahead of us, thousands had arrived after us.

As it turned out, being first in line didn't matter much. When the compound gate finally opened, late that morning, **all semblance of** a "line" disappeared. People began jostling and shoving until the line dissolved into one big, **boiling, chaotic horde**. The Americans had moved their operation out here to the wilderness, but they had not figured out a way to conduct the process peacefully.

The police evidently knew this chaos was going to break out. They must have been waiting someplace nearby, because they arrived on the scene within a few minutes to restore order. They blew their whistles and shouted commands, but no one paid any attention to them. People didn't care if the body blocking their way to the gate belonged to a policeman, they shoved the obstruction aside, whoever it was. The police swung their sticks and knocked some heads, but they were few and the refugees were many. The crowd soon overwhelmed them.

Then the army arrived. These men, too, must have been standing by, on alert. The soldiers fired their guns into the

....

all semblance of anything that looked like
boiling, chaotic horde wild crowd

air, which got people's attention, and they waded in among the people, using the butt ends of their carbines as clubs. They managed to **restore some semblance of order** and create a separation between the crowd and the compound door.

One of the Americans working inside the compound came to the gate at that point to speak to us and calm us down. "Don't fight over this," he said. "Here, we are just taking names and finding out a little about you. We will talk to every one of you, if not today, then tomorrow; if not tomorrow, then the next day. We will keep this process going as long as it takes, so be patient and let us call you in one by one."

While he stood there talking, someone in the crowd threw a stone. It hit the poor man on the head, and his forehead started to bleed. "Okay," he shouted, "that's it! The selection process is over. We're not taking any more people. You ruined it for yourselves." He went back into the compound and slammed the gate, and we could hear the clanking of metal as someone **pulled big dead bolts into place** and turned the keys in the locks.

Oh, what a wailing and howling rose then from the thousands of people assembled outside that compound! For a few hours the gate remained closed. Here and there, some commotions broke out, but the army men were standing there with their guns, and no one dared to go up against them. Mostly, people just collapsed where they had been standing and wept and cursed whoever had thrown the stone. And the vendors moved busily among the people, selling fruit juice,

....

restore some semblance of order calm the crowd
pulled big dead bolts into place locked the doors

selling ice cream.

Finally, some of the white-haired elders among the Afghan refugees knocked timidly on the compound door and pleaded through the metal of the gate, pleaded to speak to the American officials. A few of them were admitted at last. They went inside, and I can imagine what they said: *Don't punish all the people for the **transgression** of just one. Look at how the people are suffering out there. Don't send them away disappointed. Start the process again.*

The Americans relented and agreed to resume the interviews, but only if the refugees would behave themselves. After that, **under the watchful eyes of the soldiers**, people tried to restrain themselves. Even so, each time the gate opened, a **mass** moved toward the opening like a wave gathering to crash against a rocky shore. It reminded me of the border station between Afghanistan and Pakistan.

Here, however, every time the gate opened, two or three people got through. No one had to pay a bribe. In that way it was different from the border. People could see that slowly, slowly, they actually were taking applications. So even though we got nowhere near the gate that day, we had some hope that our turn might come if we returned often enough.

Well, the next morning we arrived at four A.M., an hour earlier than the day before. Yet again, hundreds of people had arrived ahead of us. As we talked to some of those people, we learned that most of them had been here all night. Some had arrived the night before and had camped in the field. Others had gotten here yesterday and had never departed.

....

transgression mistake, sin

under the watchful eyes of the soldiers while the soldiers watched

mass large crowd

Once again, however, it didn't matter who had arrived early or late. It only mattered how aggressive a person was—and how strong. Again, on this second day, I couldn't get to the front. I could only get close enough to see **how the system worked**. When the man came out, he pointed to the first person he saw. In order to be chosen, you had to be right there where **his glance could fall on you**. I kept trying that day, pulling my mother along, squirming and jostling our way forward, but I wasn't strong enough to compete. Once I got tired, I couldn't even hold our space. In the thickest middle of the crowd, bodies crushed in on us from every side. My mother couldn't breathe. We had to fight to move back the way we had come, away from the door, back to where the crowd thinned out.

My throat was **parched** and my tongue felt like shoe leather. At mid-afternoon, as often happens in Quetta in the summer, wind began to scream between the hills. These windstorms turn day to dusk with the brown dust they whip up. Once this wind started up, we could do nothing but crouch with our backs to it, covering our faces with our head scarves. That's how we all spent the next few hours, the many thousands of us assembled around that compound, men, women, children, and bawling babies. Yet, the whole time, the officials in the compound kept coming out every few minutes, kept calling refugees inside to process them.

On the third day we made our way pretty far forward early on. Suddenly, a man came out, and I saw that he was a Pakistani, not a foreigner. "Today we're taking the wounded

....

how the system worked what had to be done
his glance could fall on you he could see you
parched dry

and disabled first," he announced, and he stood there, looking out over the sea of people.

His eye fell glancingly on me. I waved my arm to hold his gaze and hobbled a step or two forward. "You there," he called out. "Yes, you." His stare remained fixed on me. "Come forward, girl. Come." The crowd had to part to let my mother and me through. He said, "What is your story?"

I told him I had stepped on a land mine as a child. My mother said nothing, standing next to me, gasping like a fish out of water, barely able to stand upright. "All right," said the man. "You two can come inside." As I slipped past him into the compound, he picked out several others from the crowd as well. We all went through the gate.

Inside the yard, I saw one small hutlike structure. Otherwise, it was just an empty field, exactly the same as the desert landscape outside. In front of the hut a man sat at a simple desk, with an open **ledger** in front of him and a box of papers next to him. He gestured to a row of unpainted wooden benches against the wall and went back to **marking figures** in his book. We sat on that bench, **our hearts booming**, awaiting the next event, scarcely daring to believe we had actually gotten inside the compound, trying to keep our fears quiet and our hopes from going wildly out of control.

At last he began calling people over, one by one. When our turn came, we stood before his table. He asked our names and wrote them down. He asked where we came from and where we lived now, and he wrote this information down. He asked how

....

His eye fell glancingly on me. He noticed me.
ledger notebook
marking figures writing numbers
our hearts booming very excited

many were in our family and who they were. My mother began to cry. I told the man that it was just the two of us, that we had lost everyone else. He nodded.

Then he handed me a slip of paper with some writing on it. "Sister-dear," he said, "here in this yard, we only make appointments. You must go to this address in Quetta for your actual interview. Go there on the day and at the time marked on this bit of paper."

Since I couldn't read, I had to ask him to read me the address and tell me the time. I memorized it.

"Don't be late," the man told me, "because you won't get another chance. Be sure to have this appointment slip with you when you go, because when you show up in that neighborhood, the police might stop you and ask what are you doing there, what is your business. If you don't have this slip of paper to show them, they will drive you away. For the same reason, don't go the day before your appointment, or the day after, or on any day except the one marked on your slip. When the time comes, be ready to answer all questions about your life and your situation. If God wills it, sister, you and your mother will go to America."

In this **courteous manner**, addressing himself first to me and then to my mother, the man **dismissed us**. He was a decent man. We thanked him and made our way out the back of the compound, through a separate door. We had to wait a few hours for the Suzuki to take us back to the city, and we never went back to that field again, although I'm told they continued to **take names** there for another month or so. But we had finished

....

courteous manner nice way
dismissed us told us to leave
take names interview others

that part of the process—we had no reason to go back there.

On our appointed day we asked directions to the address written on the slip of paper we had been given. Those directions took us to the agency's original office in that posh neighborhood. This time no crowds or commotion **troubled the atmosphere of** the neighborhood, because no one could enter that area without an official appointment slip, and only a few people had appointments at this office at any given time.

It was a stylish building on a quiet street, and if it had a sign of any kind, I don't remember it. In any case, I was not **on the lookout for** signs since I would not have been able to read them anyway. I assumed we were entering the American embassy. The Pakistani man who admitted us led the way to a room furnished only with carpets and chairs. Four or five other families were there already, waiting. Our appointment slip said eleven a.m., and we had arrived with time to spare, but they didn't call my name until about three that afternoon. I didn't mind the waiting itself—the room was comfortable; I just had trouble **holding my tensions down** all that time because I didn't know what they would ask. I didn't know if they would accept us or reject us.

A well-dressed, middle-aged, businesslike Pakistani woman conducted the interview.

"What is your name?" she asked.

I told her.

"And your mother's name?"

I answered this.

....

troubled the atmosphere of affected
on the lookout for paying attention to
holding my tensions down staying calm

"Where are you from?"

I told her, and she wrote it down.

"How did you get here? What family do you have? Why did you come to Pakistan? Why do you want to go to America?"

I said, "I want to go to America so I can get an education and **make something of my life**. Here, I have no one except my mother, and she is not well. My missing leg is a problem, too. I think we can both get better medical treatment in America. That's another reason I want to go—but mostly because I want to have a life."

The woman nodded and jotted notes. "Okay," she said. "That's fine. But we need to talk to you again. Come back in two weeks. If you don't show up for any reason, you will **be eliminated from consideration**. Here is your appointment slip."

She gave us a slip of paper with a new date and time marked on it. We came back two weeks later and went through the same procedure again. She seemed pleased with our answers, but at the end of the session she said she had to see us yet again. No American ever interviewed us. In fact, it was always the same woman, and she interviewed us four times in all. Maybe she slipped some new questions into each interview, but if so, I didn't notice. To me, it seemed like she asked the same questions every time, and I gave the same answers.

I suppose someone was **drawing up a list** based on these interviews. Maybe a few people were eliminated each time somehow. Perhaps some American official we didn't know about

....

make something of my life live a good life

be eliminated from consideration not be given another chance

drawing up a list choosing people

was reviewing the Pakistani woman's notes after each interview. I don't know. In any case, after the fourth interview she said, "Congratulations. You have been accepted. Now you have to go to the American embassy in Islamabad. They must interview you, too. If they say yes, then you will go to America."

BEFORE YOU MOVE ON...

1. **Summarize** Reread pages 155–158. What did Farah say to her mother that convinced her to go to America?

2. **Sequence** Reread pages 165–169. Farah and her mother were invited into the compound. What happened next?

LOOK AHEAD Read to page 186 to find out what happens on the way to the American embassy.

Sojourn in Islamabad

Islamabad is about a hundred miles southeast of Peshawar, and Peshawar, you may remember, is a two-day journey by train from Quetta. Getting ourselves to this distant city for an interview would cost money, and we would have to make the journey alone, two unprotected women, just as we had done in the other direction three years earlier, when we were fleeing the horrors and losses of our life in Kabul. The Taliban still controlled Afghanistan, and they still **held sway** in that region along the border, particularly around Peshawar.

But the woman who interviewed us in Quetta said **there was no way around it**. She gave us another slip of paper. "Here is the address of the American embassy in Islamabad, and here is the name and address of a nearby hotel. When you

---

held sway had control
there was no way around it we had to go to Islamabad

get to Islamabad, go directly to this hotel. In the morning make your way to the embassy. If they accept you, they will give you some money to **cover your expenses back** to Quetta. But getting from here to Islamabad in the first place—that is your responsibility. I hope you find a way, because even though *we* have accepted you, we can't send you to America without **clearance** from the embassy. So everything depends on getting to this appointment and, of course, on saying the right things when they talk to you. May God help you in your interview."

She left unsaid the other outcome her words implied: If the embassy rejected us, we would not only lose our chance to go to America, but we would have to fund our own journey back to Quetta.

Well, we scrimped, saved, and borrowed every rupee we could muster. We managed to collect enough to pay for our train tickets plus a little more for expenses and unexpected emergencies. We left with about a thousand rupees in all—the equivalent of about twenty dollars, I think.

We boarded that horrid train and headed north, two days, two nights, just like before, plus another three or four hours after Peshawar. We had never been to Islamabad before, but after three years in Pakistan we knew our way around the culture. We were not so afraid this time. The hungry-looking men with the big turbans and the kohl-rimmed eyes did not frighten us anymore, because we were used to people who looked like that. We knew it wasn't what a man wore or how he painted his eyes that made him a Talib, but what smoldered in

....

cover your expenses back pay for you to go

clearance permission

She left unsaid the other outcome her words implied: She did not suggest this:

his heart. This time we embarked on our journey with a little more confidence, saying to each other, "We'll make it."

As soon as we arrived in Islamabad, we **hailed** a taxi and gave the driver the address of that hotel.

The cabbie was an Afghan himself, and he **took a shine to** us. But he knew all about the program to take a thousand widows to America. As soon as he saw two poor females in Muslim head scarves heading for an upscale, Western-style hotel, he said, "Ooh! By Allah, you two are in that program. You definitely have money." Then he told us how much the ride to the hotel would cost.

We could not **haggle with him**. He offered to take us the long way so we could see the sights; he promised to carry our bags for us, to come for us in the morning, to ferry us all day long—in short, he offered all sorts of favors and extra services, but on the price he would not budge. "You're going to America," he insisted. "I'm doomed to spend the rest of my life in this hellhole, driving a cab. How can you deny me my just fare?"

Finally, we said, "Oh well, whatever you say. As long as you get us to this place."

So he started driving. About ten minutes from the hotel a motorcycle started following us. Two Pakistani policemen were riding on that one motorcycle. They pulled the taxi over. One of the officers came over, leaned down, and stared at us through the window. **We shrank from his gaze**, huddling into the corner. He could tell at a glance that we hailed from some other town. He could tell we were frightened, too. He asked the

---

hailed got, signaled

took a shine to liked

haggle with him get him to lower the price

We shrank from his gaze We were afraid of him

driver, "Where are you taking these people?"

The driver said, "To a hotel near the American embassy. They have an appointment there in the morning."

The policeman's lips **curled in scorn**. "Where are you from?" he asked my mother, but she was too terrified to speak. "Where are they from?" he demanded of the driver.

"They've come up from Quetta, sir. They're Afghans."

"I thought so." The policeman reached through the window and got a grip on my arm. "Where are your **passports**?" he demanded.

"Passports?" I **stammered**. We had no passports. We fled Afghanistan without paperwork, crossed the border by the smugglers' route. What did we know about passports! "We have no passports! We've come to see someone at the American embassy. They are going to interview us."

It was the wrong answer. He tightened his grip. "Give me money."

"What money? We are poor. We have no money to give you!"

"And yet you think you're going to America? You didn't come all this way without a penny. You have money, all right. Who do you think you're dealing with, some country fool? Give me everything you have."

I could not answer him. **I felt a lump in my throat.** I could feel our thousand rupees against my side, a square lump of folded bills.

The policeman let go of my arm. He told the taxi driver,

....

curled in scorn smiled meanly
passports official papers
stammered asked weakly and nervously
I felt a lump in my throat. I felt like crying.

"Follow me to the station. I have to take these people to jail. They're going to prison. No passports! That's illegal. Damn Afghans. Think they can get away with anything."

Then the driver leaned over the seat to talk to us in a lowered voice. "Auntie-dear," he said to my mother. "Why are you holding back? Give this man the money. He will never let you go until he gets it. Don't worry about the fare from the hotel to the embassy. I'll take you for free. But you have to give this man his money right now, or we're both in trouble. I know it's hard, but do it. Just give him what he wants, and this will be over."

My lips felt like ice. To be stranded in Islamabad without a penny—I could not bear the thought. My heart was **galloping in panic**.

"Come on, come on," the policeman growled. "Listen to your driver, he's a man of sense. I need eight hundred rupees, ladies. Dig into your pockets. I know you've got that much."

Then the driver **interceded** for us. "Your Excellency," he said to the policeman, "you do a hard job, patrolling these streets. Where would we citizens be if not for men like you, keeping order? God knows you're entitled to your money and plenty of it, but these are poor people. Very poor. Surely you can see that. Forgive them just this once. They'll both have passports to show you next time. Let them pay you four hundred rupees. You will earn favor with Allah for your generosity."

The policeman kept glancing over his shoulder nervously

....

galloping in panic beating fast in fear
interceded spoke

at his companion, who was still on the motorcycle. Finally, he said, "All right, all right. I don't know why I **have such a soft heart**, it will be the ruin of me, but all right. Give me four hundred rupees, and I'll let you off with a warning. No more running about the streets without proper documents, though, you hear? It's prison for the both of you next time, if I catch you. Just be thankful you ran into me instead of some hard-hearted crook of a policeman. Now hurry up with that money."

I managed to separate the demanded amount of rupees from our bills without letting the policeman glimpse **the whole roll**. He grabbed the cash and went back to his vehicle. Our new best friend, the taxi driver, then delivered us to our hotel.

It was a beautiful hotel, clean and sparkling—foreigners stayed there. As soon as we walked through the door, a man in a uniform stopped us and asked what we wanted. I told him our names and showed him the document the agency in Quetta had given us, the one that noted our appointment with the embassy and the name of this hotel. The man studied our paper and then went to his desk and checked some books. Apparently, the hotel had been told to expect us. They had our names on some list. Another man came scurrying up and tried to take our bundles, but we wouldn't give them up. He shrugged, led the way to an elevator, and then took us upstairs. He showed us into a **well-furnished** room that was just for us. It had two nice beds and its own little bathroom, which we didn't have to share with anyone.

The attendant told us if we wanted food, we could call

....

have such a soft heart am being so kind
the whole roll how much money we had
well-furnished nice

a certain number on the phone and they would bring us a meal. On the other hand, if we wanted to go downstairs to the restaurant, they would give us food there.

My mother and I got settled. We tried out the beds and washed up in the bathroom. My mother didn't want to go downstairs. "Something might happen," she faltered. She felt safer eating in the room, so I called the number and asked that our dinner be **sent up**.

A few minutes later a man came to our door with two trays of Pakistani food—lentils, rice, and meat. I could see that he had simply brought us the remains of other guests' meals. I had seen such trays of leftovers sitting outside the doors of other rooms on our way upstairs originally. Clearly, this man had **consolidated several plates of leftovers** for each of us.

I said no. I said, "Bring us a proper meal."

The waiter frowned. "This is perfectly good food. Who are you to **turn your nose up at it**?"

"When the other guests order dinner, do you bring them somebody's leftovers?"

"Well, no," he admitted. "But they are paying guests. And foreigners."

But I thought back to our arrival. The moment they accepted us into this hotel just from seeing our names on a slip of paper and showed us to our room without asking for money, I knew that someone was paying for all this. And if they were paying for the room, surely they had paid for the meals as well. I said to myself, *The hotel has already collected money to serve us*

....

sent up delivered to our room

consolidated several plates of leftovers combined what was left from other people's meals

turn your nose up at it say it is not good enough

176

meals, but now they are trying to save on the costs. So I held my ground. I refused to accept the leftovers of someone else's meal. I told the man to take the food away. "We are guests like any other at this hotel. You have to treat us the same as you treat all the other guests. Bring us the same meal you give the others. In fact, if you have a restaurant downstairs, you must have a choice of meals, so bring me a menu."

The waiter could not say anything to this because I had guessed correctly. The hotel had accepted payment for our meals, and now they were trying to avoid serving us the food. They thought we were **too ignorant to notice or too humble to protest**. Well, they were wrong about me. The waiter took away the trays of used food and came back with a menu. Unfortunately, I did not know how to read, so I made the waiter read the items to me out loud. Then I said, "Bring me this. Bring me that." My mother and I got what we wanted. We went to bed well fed, slept on soft beds, and woke up in the morning wonderfully refreshed, although tingling with nervous doubts about our interview.

Downstairs we found our taxi driver friend waiting for us. He had asked what time we had to be at the embassy before leaving us the day before. Now he drove us to the embassy and agreed to wait outside till we were done, so he could drive us back to the hotel. He charged us, of course, but why shouldn't he? He made his living that way. He still **helped us immensely**. With him in charge, we didn't have to worry about getting around a strange city, getting lost, missing our

....

too ignorant to notice or too humble to protest too stupid or shy to complain

helped us immensely really helped us

appointment. We could relax, or at least we could focus on the anxiety we felt about the interview.

At the embassy we were shown into a very grand office, where a Pakistani woman interviewed us. She asked the familiar questions. Who were we, how many, why did we want to go to America? Then she sent us to another plushly furnished room to wait. **The minutes crawled by.** At last that same woman came back and said, "Congratulations. Your application has been approved."

Our mouths dropped open. I was hoping my ears had not heard her wrong, hoping my mind had not deceived me, hoping this was not a dream. We stood up **in a daze** and followed the Pakistani woman deeper into the embassy. There, in yet another office **of dazzling grandeur**, we met the Pakistani woman's boss, a white-haired American lady. She was sitting behind an enormous desk, a desk polished to such a gleam that her reflection showed in it as it would in water. She stood up when we came in and reached out to shake our hands.

"Congratulations," she said. "You're going to America." Then she and the Pakistani woman took us to another room to look at a video about America. Three other Afghan families were there, too, all families who had just been accepted into this program. The video was supposed to **orient us to** America and let us know what to expect. First it showed typical scenes of American life—cities, streets, stores. It showed escalators and warned us not to wear long head scarves in America, nor *chadaris*, for these garments might get caught in escalator steps

....

The minutes crawled by. Time passed very slowly.
in a daze without thinking; shocked
of dazzling grandeur that was beautiful
orient us to teach us about

and strangle us. The tape then showed Afghan families just like us arriving at an airport in America and people waiting for them with big signs that said WELCOME in both English and Farsi lettering. This was how we would be greeted when we arrived in the United States, the tape seemed to say.

An Iranian man acted as narrator in this film. He and his family had gone to America as refugees. Now they lived in a nice apartment. The man led a video tour of his own home to show us what kind of life we would have in America. He showed the yard where his children played after school. The camera followed him into a living room filled with comfortable furniture, a television set, and other **amenities**. Next, he showed us his family's kitchen, which had every modern appliance one could imagine. He opened the refrigerator to show that it was full of food. My mother watched all of this in wide-eyed wonder. For the first time she began **tremulously** to believe that we might be doing the right thing, going to America. She thought they were saying they would put us in an apartment like this and give us all these things as soon as we arrived.

After the video was over, the American woman told us, "Now go home to Quetta, you two, and wait. It will take some time to complete your paperwork and **make all the arrangements**, but don't worry: As soon as your tickets come through, we will be in touch. I know you may be feeling some anxiety now. You have been through a lot, but that's in the past. All you need now is patience. You are certainly going to America."

....

amenities nice things
tremulously slowly
make all the arrangements organize your trip

The Pakistani woman translated all this for us and took down my mother's cousin's phone number so that she could reach us when the time came. Then the American lady handed my mother an envelope. "This is **train passage** back to Quetta," she said, "and you'll find some spending money in there, too, enough to cover your expenses on the way home. You can stay at the hotel one more night—the tickets are for tomorrow's train—but make sure to **check out** before noon, because otherwise, you might be charged for another night, and if that happens, you will be responsible for the bill."

My mother immediately gave the envelope to me for safekeeping. We managed to stammer out some words of gratitude and stumble out of the embassy in a daze. Our faithful taxi driver was waiting for us on the street. "Well?" he demanded. "Well? What happened, sister? Did your **petition** please the Americans?"

I did not want to say that we had been accepted into this program and were definitely going to America, just in case something should still go wrong. "It's in God's hands," I replied. "In any case, our business here is done. We go back to Quetta in the morning."

We paid our driver well for taking us back to the hotel, since we could afford it now, and he promised to come for us again in the morning.

He kept his word. We headed for the station around ten the next morning. On the way my mother said we should stop somewhere for **provisions**. She wanted to buy all the food we

....

train passage money for the train
check out leave your hotel room
petition application, request
provisions food and supplies

needed on our long journey now, so we would not have to spend money in public during the trip—the sight of cash might tempt someone to rob us.

Our driver took us to a good bazaar, and we browsed around, got some juice, got some bread, some dried fruits, a bit of this, a bit of that. By the time we finished shopping and got back in the taxi, the traffic had **thickened**. We did not know that Islamabad had a **rush hour** at midday. Now that rush hour had come upon us. The taxi could hardly move. It inched through the streets. The driver could do nothing. Finally, we reached the station. The cabbie helped us get our bundles out of the cab, entrusted us to the care of Allah, and generally lavished his best wishes upon us. We had grown fond of each other over those two days, and I believed in the sincerity of his warm wishes for us. In any case, he got back into his taxicab and drove away, and we never saw that man again.

We went into the station and inquired about our train. Which was our gate, when did the train depart? People laughed at us. "Do you mean the train to Quetta? Why, that's gone! You just missed it!"

We panicked. We ran out to the street to look for our cabdriver again, wanting somebody's advice, anybody's. But he had disappeared by then, of course. Having dropped us off, he had no reason to hang around the station.

We scuttled back indoors and showed our tickets to the man at the counter. When was the next train? we wanted to know. He **pushed his spectacles up** his nose to look through the

....

thickened become busier
rush hour lot of traffic
pushed his spectacles up put his glasses on

bottoms of them as he studied our tickets. "Not till tomorrow. There's only one a day. But these tickets are no good now. They were for today's train. You'll have to buy new tickets."

Stunned by these words, we retreated from the ticket window to **consider our situation**. My mother had gone pale. "What are we to do? Where can we go?" she moaned. "Is there another cab? Can we go back to the hotel?"

She knew the answer to that question already, but even so, I reminded my mother of what the woman had said to us at the embassy. No, we couldn't go back. The embassy had paid for only two nights. A third night would **be on us**, and we couldn't afford the rates. In fact, we couldn't afford a hotel of any kind, for we had spent most of the money the embassy had given us on provisions for the journey. My mother sank down onto her bundle and started wailing in despair. I put my arms around her and tried to comfort her, but when I felt that frail body of hers shaking and trembling in my bony embrace, my own heart dissolved and I started to cry, too. There we sat in the middle of that crowded train station, helplessly crying our hearts out.

Just then what should I see through my tears but another of those Pakistani policemen strolling toward us! And we still had no passports, no papers of any kind. Too late I thought, *Why, oh why, didn't I ask the embassy for some sort of document?* Surely they would have given me a note of some sort, saying something like, *Don't harass this girl or her mother; they are under the protection of the United States.* Too late now: The policeman was **only paces away**. He would take us to prison. And we had come so close, so

---

consider our situation think about what to do next

be on us cost us money

only paces away very close to us

close to getting on that plane to America! What could we do? He was standing over us now—a tall and handsome man. Very sturdy, very muscular. "Four-shouldered," we called such men in Kabul. "What's wrong?" he asked.

I couldn't find my voice to tell him that we had no money, that we couldn't pay him. **The words caught in my throat.** It would have been a lie anyway—we did have a little bit of money. I could only think, *Oh, please, don't take the little we have.*

"What's wrong?" he kept saying. "Why are you crying? Tell me."

Finally, his tone of voice got through to me. I realized that this man was not trying to arrest us, nor was he demanding money. He wanted to know what trouble we were in. He wanted to help. Still, I could hardly get the words out through my sobs, and my mother did no better. But eventually, choking out a phrase here and a word there, we gave him enough fragments that he was able to **piece together an idea of** our problem. "Calm down, calm down," he said compassionately. "**All is not lost.** Let us discuss this without tears and see what is to be done. What is it you really need? A ticket? Do you need a ticket for tomorrow's train to Quetta? All right. Give me the one you have, and I will talk to the stationmaster. Come with me."

Then we followed him to the ticket counter, and he spoke firmly to the man. "These women have come a long way. Due to a traffic jam, they missed their train. They have no more money. Come, come, sir: Do the right thing. Stamp the tickets they have—renew them for tomorrow. What does it cost you?

....

The words caught in my throat. I could not speak.
piece together an idea of understand
All is not lost. It will be OK.

The money has already been paid. If there is no seat, they will sit on the floor."

Finally, the train official gave in and stamped our tickets. Then the policeman led us to the back of the station. There, he showed us a row of tiny rooms that the station rented to stranded travelers, just so they would have a safe place to sleep. Of course, the station usually collected rent, but the policeman let us have one of these little rooms for free. The better rooms had beds in them. Ours was just a cubicle, but we were grateful to have that. We slept on the bare floor, with our bundles as pillows and our head scarves as our only blankets. But at least we had a door to shut, a lock to turn, a safe corner to curl up in. We got some sleep that night.

And it just **goes to show that you can never tell**. I feared that policeman on sight, because of his outfit, because of what the other policeman had done to us. But this one showed us nothing but compassion, he extended his hand to us, he comforted our grieving, and he gave us a place to sleep. You just can't tell.

We woke up early the next morning, around six or seven. The train did not leave till noon, but believe me, we didn't **stir from** the station. When the train opened its doors, we boarded and returned to Quetta **without incident**. The journey that had seemed so impossibly difficult three years ago seemed easy this time. We settled into our old life and waited for a phone call from the embassy.

This was in August of 2001.

....

goes to show that you can never tell means that you cannot assume everyone will hurt you

stir from leave

without incident with no trouble

Several weeks later we woke up to the news of September 11: Terrorists had hijacked four planes in the United States—they had destroyed famous buildings in New York, they had crashed a plane into the Pentagon in Washington, D.C., and they had killed thousands of Americans.

We placed a frantic phone call to that agency in Quetta. Would this affect our flight? we wanted to know.

They said, "What flight? All flights to America have been canceled. As for that program to take a thousand Afghan widows to America—forget it. Osama bin Laden has **turned the word 'Afghan' into mud**. We don't know when things will change, if ever."

The next week the embassy finally called us. "Unpack your bags," they said. "No one is going to America. We'll be in touch if anything changes."

In those few weeks before September 11, when we thought we were going to America, **our lives bloomed with** so much happiness, so much hope. We were not afraid to dream when we closed our eyes, confident that our dreams would give us pleasure. After September 11 my mother said, "Well, that's the end." We grew listless. We went through our days like dead people who could still somehow walk. Nothing seemed to matter.

And yet, deep down, I never lost **that kernel of certainty**. I had seen that star fall from the sky. I believed that God had shown me his power for a reason. He had shown me that he could take the mightiest life and plunge it into hell, and he

....

turned the word 'Afghan' into mud made Afghans look like bad people

our lives bloomed with we felt

that kernel of certainty hope

could take the most wretched of beings and lift her to heaven. He could do anything. And I felt sure he would.

And indeed he did. Six months **crept by, and I don't know what wheels were turning** during that time, but in the seventh month we got a second message from the embassy. The program was on again; we should pack our bags. Tickets would be delivered to us. We would fly from Quetta to Islamabad the very next week, and from there, we would go on to America. It happened so suddenly! It felt like a miracle!

And now, when I look back, the first fourteen years of my life feel like a dream—everything that happened up to the moment when I boarded the plane for America. And I still feel how important it is to pay attention to God, to recognize God, to believe in God, to live with a pure heart and **let only purity and truth come pouring from one's soul**: That's the way to live. Such is my belief.

....

crept by, and I don't know what wheels were turning passed, and I don't know what happened

let only purity and truth come pouring from one's soul do your best to be good and honest

BEFORE YOU MOVE ON...

1. **Problem and Solution** A policeman stopped Farah's taxi on the way to the embassy hotel. How did they get past him?

2. **Cause and Effect** Farah was afraid of the policeman she met in the station. What caused her feelings to change?

LOOK AHEAD Read to page 206 to find out why Farah and her mother are afraid in America.

Arriving in America

⬥

Five of us Afghan families left Islamabad for America that day in April 2002. We traveled together and got to know one another and became friends. One family consisted of a widower and his daughter. The other three were **headed by** widows, each of whom had four or five children, including some boys. Ours was the only family with no male members.

The airplane landed briefly in Holland and then went on to New York. There, we **disembarked** and were met by a small **delegation of people who took us through customs**. One of them was an Afghan; the rest were Americans. In Islamabad the embassy had given us some plastic bags with special insignias on the outside. We had been told to display these bags prominently when we arrived in America, so that the

....

headed by led by

disembarked got off the airplane

delegation of people who took us through customs group of people who helped us complete paperwork and enter the country immigration officials would know who we were and not arrest us as terrorists. The bags contained all the official documents we needed to enter the United States.

After we **got through the entry procedures**, the delegation split us into two groups. Four of the families were in one group, we were the other. The four families were all going to leave the airport, go to a hotel, and get a good night's sleep. The next morning they would all board a plane for California.

My mother and I, however, were going to get back on a plane and go to Chicago that same night. My mother panicked and protested. She wanted to do whatever the other Afghans were doing. If they were going to California, she felt we should go to California.

"That's just not where you've been placed," the Afghan fellow told us. I think he worked for World Relief, and he tried to **allay our fears**. "Chicago and California are both good. There is no difference. One place is not better than the other. It's just a matter of where you have been placed."

My mother did not believe him. "It's because we don't have a man in our family," she told me bitterly. "The families with males get to go to a hotel. Those families get to go to California. We're just women, so they're not going to let us rest. If only we had a man in our family, they would let us go to California, too. But, no! We're just women, so they're sending us to Chicago."

We had gotten very little sleep on our long journey from Pakistan, and we got no sleep at all on **that last leg** from

....

got through the entry procedures showed the documents
allay our fears calm us
that last leg the last part of the trip

New York to Chicago. My mother couldn't sleep because she now had a bad feeling about our fate. She felt something going wrong. I couldn't sleep because I knew that as soon as we landed, I would have to begin **dealing with** whatever awaited us, and I didn't know what that would be.

It was the middle of the night when we landed. We came off the plane, and I thought, *Allah help us! Look at these lights! Look at this hurrying **multitude**! Look at the stores piled high with glittering merchandise. Look at these buildings, these gleaming floors, these paintings, this abundance, this bustle, this confusion! Listen to the announcements echoing and booming out of loudspeakers we can't see!*

My mother and I felt like ants in this vast universe of an airport. We looked about for people holding signs that said WELCOME in Farsi and English, but we saw no such people. We didn't know where to find our bags and boxes containing the **meager possessions** we'd managed to accumulate in Pakistan over the years. The other passengers coming off the plane streamed around us, **full of purpose**. Two businessmen in almost identical suits caught my notice. "Let's follow them," I said. "They must be going to find their bags, so let us go there, too."

My mother had no opinion of her own about what to do. She clung to my arm and let me make all the decisions. We followed the businessmen down one corridor and up another. It was hard to trail them because it turned out there were other businessmen quite similar to them striding along the corridors. In those crowds I was afraid we would lose sight of

....

dealing with coping with, accepting

multitude crowd

meager possessions few things

full of purpose knowing where to go

our businessmen and follow two others. We had to hurry to stay close to them. My mother had trouble walking that fast. She kept begging me to slow down, but I said, "No. They're walking fast, we have to walk fast, too. We have to find our boxes. If anyone is going to meet us, that's where they will be waiting for us."

Well, we came at last to the room where passengers were picking up their luggage. We found the crowd that had come off our plane, and we waited with them. Eventually, we found all our bags, bundles, and boxes.

After that we didn't know what to do. We did not speak the language, we could not read the signs, and we did not know the rules of this place. Here, too, we looked for people holding some kind of welcome sign and didn't see them. As it turned out, the **caseworker** from World Relief had gotten caught in a traffic jam or something. She was fully intending to be there when we arrived, but she was late.

There we stood, therefore, **bewildered**, as the other passengers claimed their baggage and departed. The two businessmen went away, and we let them go, because I knew we could do ourselves no further good by following them. We stood there among the mighty buildings and the bright lights, wearing exactly the clothes we customarily wore in Pakistan and before that in Afghanistan. We had our head scarves, our veils of modesty, wrapped tightly around our heads and chins and shoulders. In Pakistan wrapping ourselves this way gave us some anonymity, some protection from stares. Here, dressed in

....

caseworker employee
bewildered confused

this manner, we stood out like ants in a sugar bowl. No one else looked the way we did. Everyone who passed by slowed down to stare at us. Finally, my mother started to cry, just like she did in that train station in Islamabad.

I started to cry, too. What were we doing here? Why had I insisted on this journey? How could we possibly make our way and **secure a place for ourselves in this mighty maelstrom of a world**? This was all my fault!

Just then, far away, I saw two people hurrying toward us, their eyes fixed on only us. They waved as they came forward, and I **caught my breath**. I said, "We're saved. Those are the people who were supposed to meet us." I would not have known them, but I suppose they recognized us the moment they saw two women wearing Muslim head scarves and sitting on makeshift boxes, holding bundles tied with twine on their laps, crying their eyes out. They knew at once that they had found their clients from Afghanistan.

Our caseworker, Zainab, came from Sudan. Years ago she had been a refugee like us. World Relief had brought her to America. She had **found her footing** here, gone to school, gotten her degree, and now she worked for the organization. She and her assistant greeted us. Her assistant, Aquila, was an Afghan woman, and she spoke Farsi. She let us know that we should go with them. They would take us to our new home.

We followed them in dutiful silence to a parking lot, a very long walk from the terminal. We all got into their van, Zainab and Aquila in the front, my mother and I in the back. Aquila

....

secure a place for ourselves in this mighty maelstrom of a world feel comfortable in this confusing place

caught my breath was able to breathe again

found her footing made a home

started driving. My mother ogled the sights out her window. I gaped at the sights out mine—the lights, the traffic, the immense and numerous highways curving in and out among one another, over and under, like tangles of snakes.

We had barely gotten out of the airport and into the **fast-moving current of cars** flowing toward the city when Zainab turned and handed each of us a little package. "Here," she said. "This is for you." I opened my package and found a toothbrush, a tube of toothpaste, a tiny bottle of shampoo, a miniature bar of soap, and I forget what else—basically, a few personal care items.

I immediately thought, *God is merciful! We have barely arrived, and already they are giving us these gifts!* I started to relax, thinking, *I was right. America will turn out to be like Germany.*

But then I sensed the tension next to me. My mother leaned close and whispered, "My child, why are they giving us these things?"

"These are gifts, Mama. They want us to feel welcome."

"But why give them to us here?" she wanted to know. "Why in the car? Why did they not place them in the apartment for us to find when we arrived?"

Her words confused me. "Here or there, **what's the difference?**"

"My child! Don't you see? *There is no apartment.* This is all we are getting—toothbrush, soap, a little shampoo. Where we're going, this is all we'll need!"

"What are you talking about?" I said. "No, Mama. You are worrying needlessly. These people are trying to help us. They

....

fast-moving current of cars traffic

what's the difference why does it matter

are taking us to our new home. That's what they told us in the airport."

"Oh, yes?' my mother whispered bitterly. "They would have told us anything to get us into the car."

Just then we pulled up in front of a house. Zainab got out of the van and opened my door. Aquila did the same on the other side and tried to help my mother out. At that moment, however, the people who lived in the house came out. My mother took one look at them and the blood drained from her face.

Zainab was talking to me in English, telling me that World Relief had not been able to **line up housing** for us quite yet, that a kind family had therefore volunteered to take us into their home temporarily as guests. We would be staying with them for two weeks at the most, until permanent housing could be arranged for us.

I was listening to her with all my energy, but I could piece together only the vaguest idea of what she was saying. She was speaking in English, and Aquila was on the other side of the van, trying to coax my mother out of the car, assuring her that these were good people. Suddenly, I didn't know what to believe. After our long journey and our many sleepless hours and the confusion of our arrival and the shock of being in a place so different and new, I could not think straight. I tried to reassure my mother, but my voice had no confidence, and she trusted her own fearful instincts more than my **halfhearted reassurances**. No matter what I said, she just shook her head and said, "No, my child! **The scales have fallen from my eyes.** I see the truth

....

line up housing find a home
halfhearted reassurances uncertain words of hope
The scales have fallen from my eyes. I understand now.

now. All the things our neighbors said in Pakistan were true!" Her certainty began to **sway me**. Zainab and Aquila didn't know what she was referring to, of course, but I knew, and her fear became my fear. She meant that we were going to be slaves here. There would be no comfortable house for us, no apartment of our own, no school for me, none of that. We were getting a toothbrush, a bottle of shampoo, and a new owner.

My mother started to curse me. "This was your idea," she said. "This is all your fault! *Akh!* I told you, Daughter! But you wouldn't listen, you **headstrong** girl. Oh, no—*you* knew best, you said! You had been to *Germany!*"

Aquila had taken hold of my mother's arm and was tugging gently, murmuring words of encouragement, but my mother would not get out of the car.

Meanwhile, the man and woman of this house—Mary and John, as I learned much later—were coming down the walkway, toward the van. The closer they came, the bigger they looked. We Hazaras are not a tall people. Strong, but not tall. To us, these people looked like giants. When my mother saw them looming next to the van, huge and fat and tall, her fear turned to utter terror. She tried to **yank herself out of Aquila's grip**. The assistant continued to pull on her, but she clung to her seat, to the seat belt, to anything. Zainab, half laughing, was trying to tell us, "Calm down, stop worrying, these people won't hurt you."

Somehow or other they got us out of the car and into the house. They practically had to drag us. I'm sure we woke the

....

sway me make me afraid, too

headstrong stubborn

yank herself out of Aquila's grip run away from Aquila

neighbors with our **commotion**. Mary and John lived in a nice, quiet neighborhood in the town of Glen Ellyn. I'm sure it wasn't every night that a van pulled up to their curb and a pair of trembling Afghan women were dragged, howling and resisting, up the walkway to their house.

Once they got my mother indoors, she stopped crying and protesting. She lost her voice. She just sat on the couch, where they put her, arms crossed in front of herself, hunched protectively, her scarf pulled across half her face, her eyes wild and frightened, her breath coming in rasps and gasps. I can't imagine what John and Mary thought. They were probably asking themselves at that moment why they had ever agreed to take in such houseguests. They were probably wondering how they were going to get through two weeks of hosting us.

Meanwhile, Zainab and Aquila were **taking their leave**. The hour was late, and they had completed their assignment. As they saw it, they had gotten us safely to **our place of refuge**. They told us to sleep well, assured us that they would check on us the next morning, and left us alone with the terrible giants.

These fearsome giants began chatting with us **as affably as could be imagined**, but we didn't have the eyes to see their affability. Then a very large dog came shuffling out of some other part of the house, and this beast renewed my mother's panic. In Pakistan and Afghanistan no one keeps a dog in the house. People think of dogs as unclean. We were shocked at the sight of such a creature indoors—shocked and frightened, for it came right over to sniff us and push its nose against us, and we

....

commotion noise
taking their leave saying goodbye
our place of refuge a safe place
as affably as could be imagined in kind voices

thought it was coming to bite us. When it shook itself, its hairs flew all over my mother, which was a terrible thing, though we did not know it at the time, because my mother is allergic to dog hair—a fact she had not had any opportunity to discover in the Eastern world.

The giants went on talking to us. Much later we discovered from Zainab what actually took place that night. Mary and John, **our first sponsors**, told us the name of their dog. They cheerfully assured us we had nothing to fear from the poor animal. They told us they had two children, who were asleep upstairs at this hour. They told us we had to **keep our voices down**. They said they wanted us to feel welcome. We listened to them with blank faces, hearing only sounds, not words. The giant woman said we must be hungry and asked if we would like something to eat. We heard the noise coming from her mouth and responded **with uncomprehending looks**. The man, poor fellow, brought us some milk, guessing that we would want it even if we did not admit to any hunger. He brought us some biscuits and some cookies. But my mother was trembling uncontrollably by this time. She ignored the cookies and milk, hugging herself all the more tightly, trying to warm herself up—fear makes a person cold. She was afraid of the food. She thought that at the very least it would contain ingredients forbidden by the dietary rules of Islam. She had heard, for example, that people in the West often use alcohol to make sweets, so she didn't trust the cookies. And non-Islamic ingredients were the least of her anxieties. She worried that

....

our first sponsors the first people assigned to help us

keep our voices down speak quietly

with uncomprehending looks without saying anything because we did not understand

the cookies might be laced with sleeping potion or some kind of poison.

Well, the **man of the house** went upstairs to make sure the children were still asleep and to reassure them in case the commotion had woken them up and frightened them. The wife let us know with gestures that we should follow her. She wanted to show us around the house as a way of making us feel comfortable and at home. She showed us the kitchen. She opened the refrigerator and showed us the food inside. She showed us the bathroom. She pointed out the towels and made rubbing motions to indicate that we could use these to dry ourselves after our shower the next morning. We didn't know what we were supposed to get from this tour. We just followed her around and looked at each thing she pointed to.

This family had prepared a bedroom for our use. Normally, one of their sons slept in this room, but they had put their two boys together in one room to clear this one out for us. They **ushered** us into this room now and smiled and said good night and closed the door.

We were alone. My mother looked around. She said, "Well, this is our room from now on, our prison. She **made such a point of** showing us the kitchen and the bathroom, so that's where we will be working, starting tomorrow. We'll be cleaning the bathroom and cooking for them. We'll be scrubbing the tiles. It's going to be hard work. Did you notice how spotless everything was? You'll be on your hands and knees. Nothing gets that clean by itself. I hope you're happy,

....

man of the house husband
ushered led
made such a point of was very clearly

Farah. **You got us into this.**"

We stretched out on our beds and lay awake all night, trying to figure out what **lay in store for us.** The next morning Zainab and Aquila came by. Aquila asked us why we had **put up so much resistance** the night before. My mother confessed her fears, and Aquila said to my mother, "Auntie-dear, you've got it wrong. Things like that don't go on here. Slavery is against the law in America. Perhaps you've heard stories about criminals in America—but these people are not criminals. These are good people. You were not brought here to be their slaves. This family has a good reputation. They are respected far and wide for their honor."

But who could believe such an assurance at a time like that? My mother's nerves were buzzing. She clutched that poor translator's arm. "Aquila-jan," she pleaded. "We'll go with you. Take us to your home."

But the translator said, "I'm sorry, but I don't have room for you in my small apartment. I have children of my own. Stay here for now. Be thankful that these people have **extended their generosity**. I'll phone in a couple of days to see how you're doing." And with those words, she departed.

"She's working for them!" my mother surmised gloomily. "She's in their pay. It's her job to calm us down and make us quietly accept our new role as slaves."

We went into our designated room, locked the door, and stayed inside for two days, never sleeping or eating, just moping and weeping. The family kept knocking on the door and

....

You got us into this. This is your fault.
lay in store for us would happen to us
put up so much resistance acted so afraid
extended their generosity agreed to help you

pleading with us to come out, eat something, talk to them, tell them what was troubling us.

We would not unlock the door. God only knows what they must have thought, poor folks. The second night my mother dug a scrap of paper out of her bundle. Her cousin in Quetta had given us her phone number before we left. She had asked us to phone her when we arrived in America. My mother gave me the number and said, "Late tonight, when the Americans have gone to bed, go out there and call this number. Talk to your aunt. Tell her it was all true, what people said. At least that much we can do—save others from our fate, our mistake. Tell her we need help, that we're here as slaves."

Well, that night, long after midnight, I quietly unlocked our door and stealthily crept out into the house to look for the phone. Slowly, slowly, I made my way into the kitchen, where I thought I had seen it. And indeed, there it was, a cordless phone in its cradle.

I didn't want to turn on any lights, but a weak bulb was burning in the hood above the stove, **shedding** just enough light to let me read the writing on that scrap of paper. Ignorant of the world as I was, I knew nothing about international codes, access numbers, country codes, or telephone cards. What my mother's cousin had given us was just her local number in Quetta. I tapped out those numbers and nothing happened. Then a mechanical voice said something in English. I hung up, my heart pounding. I didn't know what to do. I **darted a frightened glance** around me at the dark house. Then I picked

....

shedding shining
darted a frightened glance quickly looked

up the phone and dialed that same number again. Again, I got the mechanical voice, followed by a loud humming.

At that moment I heard a creaking sound. I looked up. The man of the house, that blond giant, was coming down the stairs. I darted back into my room, locked the door, and bent down to look through the keyhole to see if he was coming after me. I saw him pick the phone up out of its cradle and take it upstairs. This sent my thoughts skittering and squawking like chickens chased by dogs. **Suddenly, my last resistance to my mother broke.** The man had taken the phone upstairs so that we could not call anyone. I may have harbored some doubts before, but now I knew my mother was right: We were here as slaves, and we were trapped, really trapped.

My mother wanted to know if I had reached anyone. I told her what had happened. She wrung her hands and paced to the window to look out at the family's pleasant backyard.

She said, "Oh dear. Oh dear. This morning—very early, before the sun comes up, before the first light—break out of this house, Farah. You flee. The giants will still be sleeping. They won't expect you to escape then. As soon as you get outside, run like the wind. Try to get help, but if you can't get help, just keep going. Don't worry about me. I'm old, I'm going to die soon anyway. What's the difference if I die a slave or free? The main thing is for you to get away."

"Oh, Mama," I protested, "with my legs, how far would I get? How fast do you think I can go? They have police in this country. They'll send dogs after me. Even if I can get out of

....

Suddenly, my last resistance to my mother broke. I finally believed my mother's fears were true.

this house, where can I flee? I don't know anyone in America. We have to stay here and see what happens. Mama, we have no choice."

So there we stayed another night, trembling and in fear, huddled in our room. In the morning, when we heard the family stirring about in the kitchen, my mother went to the woman of the house. "Please," she pleaded, "take us back to the people who brought us here." She meant World Relief, but we didn't know the name.

She was speaking in Farsi, so poor Mary didn't know what she wanted. As it turned out, however, Mary decided to do the very thing we wanted, because she **was at her wit's end** and didn't know how to help us anymore. She took us to the World Relief office to talk to the director.

We stood by while Mary and the director talked to each other. Then the director turned to us and said some words. Probably, she was saying something like, *Why are you afraid? There's nothing to be afraid of.* But for all we knew, she could have been saying, *Enjoy these last few moments together, because tomorrow we'll be taking your mother to the soap factory.*

Meanwhile, someone in the office had phoned another Afghan they happened to know, a woman named Fatima, who had been in America for only one year. They thought that since she was almost as new as we were in America, she would understand what was troubling us. When she finally arrived and heard what had been going on, she started trying to reassure us, just as the other Afghan woman, Aquila, had done. "What are

....

was at her wit's end did not know what to do

201

you scared of? Don't be scared. America isn't like you think."

My mother said, "Well, why can't we come and stay with you?"

Fatima sighed. "All right. Please come home with me for lunch." Then she said to the World Relief director, "Let me take these two home for now, and I'll talk to them. I'll get them to understand what you're doing. They can't stay with me, though. My house is too small, but I'll talk to them and then take them back to the American sponsors. Maybe I can calm them down enough to **make this work**."

So we went home with Fatima. It was noon, so she gave us some bean stew to eat. My mother was relieved to see food she recognized, cooked by an Afghan. She trusted that it would not contain pork or liquor. It was the first meal she could eat without dread and doubt since we arrived in America. After the meal we fell fast asleep, and we were able to do this because we felt safe in Fatima's house.

At dusk our original translator, Aquila, came over. She took us all to her house for dinner. Over a good meal she told my mother, "Have patience, Auntie-dear. **Don't jump to conclusions.** You're new to this world. You must accept that some of your judgments and ideas may be mistaken. It's natural to be afraid, but before you make any decisions based on fear, take some time to get to know these people and their customs. Slowly, you will begin to understand how it is here. Then you'll **find some peace of mind**. For now, trust the people who have been here longer. Take what we're telling you on faith, because

....

make this work convince them

Don't jump to conclusions. Don't think you know about things you do not understand.

find some peace of mind know you are safe

we know how things are here and you simply don't."

So we ate with her, and then she agreed to let us stay at her house that night, but only that one night, just so we could get one good night's sleep. In the morning, she warned us, we would have to go back to the Americans.

But in the morning the sound of my mother's breathing woke me up. She was rasping like a dying woman. I knew that sound well. It meant that my mother was having an asthma attack. I jumped out of bed, yanked on my prosthesis, and rushed out to find Aquila.

Aquila called for help, and an ambulance came roaring to the house within minutes. Two men put my mother on a stretcher and rushed her out to their van.

I went running after them, shouting, "Wait for me!"

Aquila followed me out. "You can't go in the ambulance," she informed me. "Come in my car. We will follow them to the hospital."

Well, the ambulance **took off** much faster than we could go, but Aquila knew where they were going. By the time we arrived at the hospital, they had rushed my mother to a room. Aquila helped me figure out where she was. I could never have dealt with the nurses and clerks and officials in that hospital by myself. I could never have explained who I was or made known what I wanted, but with Aquila's help, we found out my mother's room number and got permission to go up there.

My mother was lying in a hospital bed, blinking and struggling for breath. Emergency medical people were

....

took off left

swarming around her. I wanted to know what they were doing and how my mother was **faring**. Was she dying? But no one had time to tell me anything. Aquila kept pulling me back. "Let them work, little one. Let them do their work."

Several hospital workers helped Aquila hold me back. With my arms restrained, I watched a doctor approach my mother with a **hypodermic**. He injected medicine into her arm, medicine that was supposed to open up her air passages, I guess. He did not know that my mother was allergic to that medicine. He never thought to ask me. I didn't know to tell him. I couldn't speak to them properly, and anyway, I figured they were doctors, so they must know what they were doing. This was America. It was like Germany. The doctors here were all experts. So I watched the man give my mother that shot, and within seconds—seconds!—her body jerked, her eyes closed, and she fell back against her pillow, to all appearances—dead.

The doctors went into a frenzy of motion, bustling about my mother, shouting orders at one another, calling for equipment and medications and I don't know what else. Hospital workers came running in, wheeling strange-looking machines with dials and knobs.

I started screaming. I tried to break away from the people who were holding me, but I couldn't do it. They dragged me out of the room. "Farah, Farah! You cannot stay in there," Aquila was telling me. "You *must* let the doctors do their work."

"What did they do to her?" I wailed. "They're supposed to be doctors. I thought they were doctors!" I really thought they

....

swarming moving quickly
faring doing
hypodermic needle

had killed my mother, and I could not contain my grief and despair. I could not tolerate being anywhere except in that room with my mother. I wanted to hold her, see her, cling to her, and never let her go.

But Aquila and the hospital workers held me in the hall. Aquila kept crooning to me, "It's okay. Your mother will be fine. Just let the doctors do their work."

A few moments later one of the medical people came out, wiping his hands on a cloth. "Tell her," he said to Aquila, "that her mother is **stable**. We've got her on a **respirator**, she's getting oxygen, and that's good. Tell her that she's still unconscious, but her **vital signs are good**."

And Aquila told me, "Your mother is sleeping. The doctor says she will be fine. You have to be patient. She'll be fine."

I didn't know what to believe, but after a while they let me into her room. I could see that she was breathing, and so she was not dead. She did look asleep. Actually, she was in a **coma**. Ordinarily, the hospital did not let patients' families stay by them twenty-four hours a day, but Aquila explained my situation to the staff, and they made an exception in my case. I can't imagine how I could have gone away and left my mother there. I can't imagine how, for instance, I could have gone back to that house in Glen Ellyn, to John and Mary's place. Fortunately, I did not have to. They put a cot next to my mother's bed, and I slept there during the night. By day I sat next to her and held her hand.

She lay unconscious for a week. Even though the doctors

....

stable out of danger
respirator breathing machine
vital signs are good body is recovering
coma deep sleep

kept saying that her "vital signs" were good and that she would probably wake up pretty soon, I lived in dread that entire week.

Then one morning she simply opened her eyes. At that moment I felt as if the roof had parted and sunshine had come pouring in. My body lost its heaviness, and I felt as if I might rise into the air.

Later that day Zainab **dropped by**. With Aquila standing by to translate, she told us, "Okay, now I understand: You don't want to stay in an American home. Well, I have some good news. We have found an apartment for you."

My mother was released from the hospital that day, and another World Relief worker named Susan Sperry took us directly to our new lodgings, a one-room apartment with a kitchenette and a bathroom. That one room had a couch, two beds, and a table.

I said, "This isn't like the apartments they showed us in Islamabad, in the video."

My mother said, "Never mind, my child. Never mind. It's a room of our own. We can come and go as we please. This means we are not to be slaves. Don't say a single complaining word. This is fine. This is wonderful."

And so we settled into a little home, where my mother could finally find some relief from the anxieties and horrors that had plagued her life for nearly twenty years.

....

dropped by visited us

BEFORE YOU MOVE ON...

1. **Conclusions** Reread pages 192–195. Farah and her mother thought they were slaves in America. Why?

2. **Cause and Effect** Reread pages 204–205. What caused Farah's mother to have problems in the hospital?

LOOK AHEAD Read to page 215 to find out about Farah's new responsibilities.

DISCOVERING
AMERICA

—◦◦◦◦◦—

We spent our first few months in America just doing paperwork and going to government offices and other agencies. All day, every day, this was our work—filling out forms, signing documents, waiting in lines, and answering questions.

Our caseworker, Zainab, helped us with all these chores, because this is what the people at World Relief do. They rescue refugees from terrible situations around the world and help them make the transition to living in America.

What we needed, first of all, was permission to stay in this country: We had to **secure refugee status**. Zainab helped us with this application. Then she helped us apply for **public aid**. Thanks to World Relief, my mother and I began receiving food stamps. We got on **social security** and started getting

....

secure refugee status get classified as people from another country who needed a safe place to live

public aid government help

social security a government program for financial help

payments for being disabled. We got into a program that allowed us to see doctors and get medical care. Eventually, World Relief helped us move to an apartment in a **subsidized** housing complex, which brought our rent down to a level we could afford on our disability payments.

Both my mother and I needed a lot of medical help in those first few months. Zainab made all our medical appointments because we didn't know who to call, what to say, how to say it, what people were saying to us on the phone, or how we were supposed to pay for anything.

We had to take taxis to and from doctor's appointments. My mother and I, however, feared those taxi drivers because they were heavy smokers and empty liquor bottles littered the backseats of their taxis. Their cabs reeked of tobacco, and they themselves puffed away on cigarettes constantly as they drove. Plus, their cabs were often covered with dog hair, which **exacerbated** my mother's lung problem. We dreaded those rides to the hospital.

Those taxi drivers always took the **most circuitous routes** to our destinations, **so as to fatten their fares**—we were not paying them, but somebody was. I got the idea that everything in America is far away from everything else. I used to think it took an hour and a half to get to my doctor's office. In truth, it takes only twenty minutes, if traffic is light.

The cabdrivers often caused problems for us by coming late. One time I had an appointment in Chicago with a prosthetics lab. They were supposed to see if I qualified to get a new

....

subsidized government-supported

exacerbated worsened

most circuitous routes longest way

so as to fatten their fares to get more money

prosthesis from them, because my original one was tattered and the wooden foot I got in Pakistan was cracking. The taxi came late. When I walked into the lab, I was scolded. "Go home!" they said. "You were supposed to be here at one o'clock, and look at the time now. We can't help you today. Make another appointment." We went back to the suburbs **with our heads hanging low**. It took over a month to get another appointment.

Even though I was only fourteen years old, everyone treated me as the **head of household**. I had become the parent, and my mother had become the child. For one thing, I had the energy to deal with all the questions that came up. For another, I began to pick up some English as soon as we arrived. Even in the car from the airport to that house in Glen Ellyn, I learned a few words. Every day, one way or another, I learned a few more phrases. In any case, I had to take charge because my mother let go of decision-making altogether. In her shell-shocked state every question bewildered her. More and more when I tried to consult her, she said, "You decide about this one, my child. You know best about such matters."

I longed to start school, but we arrived as the school year was **winding down**, and besides, I could not enter an ordinary public school until I spoke English. I asked my caseworker if there were any lessons I could start right away, and she said yes. She found a local church that was offering a course in ESL— English as a second language and signed me up for it. I went to that course from eight in the morning to twelve noon, four days a week. I studied with refugees from China, Ethiopia, Mexico,

---

with our heads hanging low feeling sad and ashamed
head of household adult in charge
winding down ending

and many other countries, people of all ages including some as young as me and others with white hair.

My mother did not want me to go to school. She begged me to stay home with her. She worried about me going anywhere by myself, but also she could not bear to be left alone in the apartment. **Solitude** frightened her. To be quite frank, everything frightened her. Deep down I always knew we were among good people here in America and that no one meant us any harm, yet even I frequently felt lost and confused. And my mother found America ever so much more **befuddling** than I. She had seen nothing of the world except the compounds of Afghanistan and the camps in Pakistan. She had no frame of reference by which to judge what was safe here in the United States and what was dangerous. All the bustle, noise, and spectacle swamped her senses, so she **hovered on the edge of panic all the time**, especially when we were out in public.

You have to realize how vastly this world differed from the one we left behind. Everything moves quickly in America. You notice this difference sharply if you have come from a slow-placed land like Pakistan. Here in America, events unfold in a flash. Outside your window, the traffic never stops zooming. On the street no one has time to answer your questions. Every person you encounter has a purpose, and although they may try to be nice, you are in the way, frankly, with your timid concerns, your clumsy questions, and your need for help.

In the grocery store people hurry up and down the aisles with their carts. They already know what they want and what

---

Solitude Being alone

befuddling confusing

hovered on the edge of panic all the time was always scared

is in each box. They don't have to guess at the contents of each package from the pictures on the outside. They can read. In the checkout line the crowd flows quickly, and you have to keep up. You never see a cashier ringing up a few items, then stopping to chat and have a cup of tea with a customer, then ringing up a few more items, then pausing to inquire about somebody's children—it never happens. If the line slows down, people get angry. It's all business here. Put your purchases on the belt; when it's your turn to pay, you had better be ready.

If you have an appointment somewhere, you have to know how to get there before you leave home. You have to know how long it takes so you can leave on time. Along the way you have to watch the clock to make sure you're on schedule. If you have never been to the place before, you are supposed to look at a map. But what if you have no map? What if you have no clue about how to use a map? What if you get lost? You're supposed to follow the signs, but what if you can't read? What if you need help in some public place and you don't speak English? You're not likely to find some random stranger there who happens to speak Farsi. **You're trapped inside your language** like a rabbit in a cage.

Every time my mother and I left the house, we felt like **hares** venturing out of our holes. We were **panting** with nervous dread. Everybody enjoys reading an adventure story or seeing an adventure movie, but a real-life adventure is harder to enjoy because you don't know how it will end. I always felt the blood pounding in my wrists when I walked out the doors of

....

You're trapped inside your language Your language limits you
hares rabbits
panting breathing hard

our apartment building.

Even a trip to the grocery store left us exhausted because we had to be alert all the time out there, on the lookout for danger—without knowing what we were looking out for. To us, everything looked unusual, everything looked menacing, so we had to watch other people to decide if there was anything to worry about. We had to be ready to do as they did. That's why going to the grocery store was such hard work mentally.

But it wasn't just a mental effort. A trip to the store **taxed us physically**, too. We lived in the suburbs, where you don't see shops on every corner. Private homes stretch on and on for blocks. When people need something, they get in a car and drive. We, however, did not have a car. We had to walk to the store, even though it was far away, and we had to go often because we could not carry very much back.

In our apartment we had just a few **sticks** of furniture. We had brought virtually nothing from Pakistan except our clothes, a few pictures, one pot, and a couple of dishes. We cooked our meals in that one pot. If we wanted to eat two things, we had to cook the first item, eat it, wash the pot, and then cook the second item. If a recipe needed two things to be cooked at once, we couldn't make it.

Nor did we have a phone. Every time we needed to call our caseworker, we had to walk to a pay phone, and in the suburbs you don't find those on every corner either. We learned to organize our life to make our phone calls at the same time we got our groceries, but sometimes an emergency **came up**—for

....

taxed us physically made our bodies tired
sticks pieces
came up suddenly happened

instance, when my mother had to see a doctor right away. On such occasions I left her at home and walked to the nearest phone as quickly as I could, and then we had to wait for that **abominable** taxi.

So even though my mother and I had achieved some **security** at last, we did not feel safe and life remained a struggle. What's more, I felt unbearably lonesome much of the time. I had no one except my mother, and my mother was not herself, not the mother I recognized. Her difficulties **still bristled**. It wasn't just her asthma. She had mental problems, too. She had trouble **making connections** or answering simple questions. She could not put two or three sentences together. She paced about our apartment with dazed eyes. Ailing, frightened, and driven into herself, she lived almost entirely inside her own head. When I came home from my English classes, she never said, *How was your day?* or *What did you learn?* She just sat silently, lost in her nightmares. I felt so alone.

World Relief tried to connect us up with other Afghans in the area, but the other Afghans led busy lives of their own. Many of them had to work two jobs just to survive. They had no time for us. Besides, they didn't know us. Two people don't automatically become friends just because they come from the same country. And we didn't know any Americans, either, so we lived an empty life, homesick by day for a world we never wanted to see again, a world we visited too often in our nightmares.

World Relief got us signed up for all the programs to which we were entitled, and that was all that they could do for us. We

....

abominable terrible, hated
security feelings of comfort
still bristled made things hard
making connections understanding things

didn't understand their limitations and guidelines at first. We thought they were going to take care of us until we no longer needed help. After three months in the United States we had not reached that point. Every day we had problems we could not handle on our own. We kept calling our caseworker.

After a certain point, however, we were not entitled to any more aid from World Relief. The organization has **a limited staff and a large mission**, and this mission does not cover caring for refugees indefinitely. World Relief needs to **conserve resources** in order to keep helping more people in more places. On their books we had now joined the list of the already-rescued. Our constant phone calls began to overburden Zainab, because she had **new clients** now. New clients arrived every week.

One day my mother wanted some meat. She would eat only *halal* meat, which is meat from an animal that has been slaughtered according to the procedures prescribed by Islam. If these rituals have not been observed, a Muslim considers the meat unclean and unfit to eat. This is one reason why my mother would not eat in most restaurants. I knew from talking to some of the other people at my English course that we could get *halal* meat from a certain Arab grocery store, but it was quite far away from our apartment. I called my caseworker and said, "We have to get to this Arab food store. My mother needs *halal* meat."

Zainab said, "Well, I can't take you there, but if you want to go to that Arab food store, go ahead. You don't need me anymore."

....

a limited staff and a large mission few employees and a lot of work

conserve resources save money

new clients other refugees to help

I did not understand. I felt abandoned—and alarmed.

Another day I called Zainab and said, "We have to make a doctor's appointment."

"Go ahead and make one," she said. "I gave you the number. Call the office." Then she told me, "Farah, World Relief has brought you as far as it can. Now you have to learn how to live in this country without our help. You have to start making your own way. Good luck."

I was stunned. I didn't know how we could make our own way without help. Probably, some families have fewer difficulties than we did. Some families have at least one person who speaks English, for example; or they have at least one person in good physical health. My mother and I just spoke Farsi, and we both had medical needs and disabilities. Every aspect of everyday life challenged us.

I didn't know what to do except to keep going to my English course and hope that no emergencies would **crop up**. If the checks had stopped coming, for example, I would not have known what to do, who to call, or what to say. I just kept a tight grip on the routines of my life and **fixed my gaze on my next step**. In my heart I held on to the belief that God would not abandon us now that he had brought us this far.

....

crop up suddenly happen

fixed my gaze on my next step tried to think about the next thing I had to do

BEFORE YOU MOVE ON...

1. **Paraphrase** Reread page 209. Farah writes, "I had become the parent, and my mother had become the child." What does she mean?

2. **Cause and Effect** Reread pages 214–215. What happened when Farah asked Zainab for help getting *halal* meat? Why?

LOOK AHEAD Read pages 216–236 to find out what happens when Farah meets an "angel."

ENTER ALYCE LITZ

⌘

June passed into July. The weather grew muggy and brown. Every day I came home from my English class exhausted from the effort of listening so hard and focusing so intensely for so many hours. Usually, as soon as I got through the door, I threw myself on my bed and fell fast asleep for a few hours.

One day I stopped to do some grocery shopping along the way, so I came home late. My leg was hurting that day, and I felt unusually anxious, although I didn't know why. I lay down, closed my eyes, and began to dream without really falling asleep. I dreamed that I was trying to **dial 911** but the phone didn't have those numbers. It had all the other numbers, but not those. I dreamed that I had to get through to emergency services because someone was at our door, knocking and

---

dial 911 call the number for emergency help

banging, and my mother had collapsed and we were alone.

The knocking finally grew so loud that I **rose out of my dozing state** and realized that this was no dream. Someone actually *was* knocking on our door. This never happened unless I had **placed a call to** our caseworker. No one ever came to see us unexpectedly, because we did not know anyone.

Well, I got out of bed, strapped on the remains of my old prosthetic leg, and opened the door. There stood Susan Sperry from World Relief, and beside her stood two other American women who were strangers to me. Blessed be the name of God, they stood there looking so blond, so tall, and so **merry**.

I invited them in and seated them on our only piece of furniture, a tattered couch. Since we had no chairs, I stood. My mother quickly brought out tea and fruit and hard candies for our guests. She had to boil the water in that one pot and serve the tea in paper cups, but still, I think my mother and I both felt delighted to have visitors. The opportunity to welcome guests into our apartment made us feel more Afghan in a good way, made us feel like we had a home.

Of course, I wondered what this was all about.

Susan introduced the women. "This is Alyce," she said of the taller woman, "and this is Lorraine. These women work with World Relief as volunteers. They want to come once a week and help you with your English. How does that sound? Would you like that?"

I watched her lips and listened as hard as I could. After almost three months in the ESL course, I knew enough English

....

rose out of my dozing state woke up
placed a call to contacted
merry friendly, happy

to **get the gist of** what she was saying. I got that these women wanted to tutor me, and I said yes enthusiastically, not just because I needed the help, but because if they tutored me, they would come to our house once a week. We would have visitors! We would get to know somebody!

The strangers then began asking me questions. They spoke very slowly and loudly because they knew that I had trouble with English. I listened hard and **more or less** understood what they were asking. I answered them, but what I said or how I said it, I don't know. I can't believe I **got anything across to them**, although when I asked Alyce about it later, she said, "You made sense. You answered all our questions. You spoke very well." I think she is **exaggerating**. She remembers me saying very clearly, "I love Mickey Mouse." I don't remember that.

I do remember that they asked me questions like, "What is your name? Where did you come from? How many are in your family—is it just the two of you? Do you have many difficulties? What do you need? How can we help?"

Somehow I managed to say, "Yes, we have many problems. First of all, with transportation, getting groceries, getting to the doctor, these are the biggest things."

Then they asked, "What do you need for your house? Do you need anything?"

Well, since we did not have anything, the answer was yes, we needed everything. But I wondered what I should say we needed if I could mention only one thing. What did we need the most? I said, "A telephone." I thought that item might make

....

get the gist of understand

more or less mostly

got anything across to them made any sense

exaggerating praising me too much

the biggest difference to everything else we did.

Then the one named Alyce opened her bag and took out some presents for us: some coloring books, a box of crayons, and a set of markers. She handed these to me. I was instantly reminded of Christina, the woman who had befriended me in Germany, for she, too, had brought me art supplies. I started coloring in the books right away, because I **was hungry for just this sort of occupation**.

You might suppose that a person who has escaped from suffering and oppression and the threat of death will be grateful and content simply to exist after that and want nothing more. But the human heart easily grows restless. It cannot stop yearning. Living in this little apartment with my mother, I had come to **long for** something more than the mere absence of pain. I had come to crave some activity that would interest my mind. I wanted some fun.

Those markers and coloring books were fun for me. I spent the whole afternoon drawing and coloring. Alyce joined in. After the visitors left us that day, I wanted them to knock on the door and start the visit all over again!

Well, Lorraine got busy with her family life, so she did not come back the following week. But Alyce came, and she brought along a telephone. She installed it for us and got the service turned on. Now, for the first time since arriving in America, we felt connected to the world we lived in.

Then Alyce asked what else we needed.

I dared to tell her that we needed pots and pans, dishes, and

....

was hungry for just this sort of occupation really wanted to do something fun

long for want

cooking **utensils**. She brought us all those items and asked, "What else?"

I couldn't believe what was happening to us. Who was this angel? I decided to go ahead and tell her everything we needed; and she brought it all.

We were still wearing our Afghan clothes up to this point, because we had no others and no money to buy any. In our Afghan clothes we **stood out** everywhere we went. People looked at us and immediately thought, *Those two are foreigners. They don't belong here.*

You can feel such thoughts on your skin. Alyce brought us clothes that matched the customs and styles of this country. We put them on, and the next time we went out, we could feel the sweet anonymity of blending in. American clothes made us feel so much safer in public.

Then one day Alyce's husband, John Litz, came over with a big television set for us. My mother says we used to have a television in Kabul, but I don't remember it. I was too little then. We saw television in Pakistan, of course, although not regularly. There, they show a lot of cricket, and we don't like cricket, because you have no idea what is going on in that game, where it begins or ends. We did like the occasional Indian movies we saw on Pakistani television, which are called "Bollywood movies" because they are made in Bombay. They feature a lot of singing and dancing. And Quetta television also showed Pakistani movies made in Lahore, which are known as "Lollywood" films.

....

utensils tools

stood out looked very different

You can feel such thoughts on your skin. You know when people are thinking this.

They are much like Bollywood films—they have the same kind of singing and dancing—and we liked those, too.

But here in America, my mother feared television. She had heard that American television features **scandalous programs filled with indecent sights unfit for the human eye**. According to people in Pakistan, the images on American television are so indecent, a single momentary glimpse of them could corrupt a young girl like me. For this reason, my mother would not let me turn on our new television at first, lest I see something harmful to me before we could switch the channel or turn off the set.

But after a hard day of studying English and struggling with the complications of living in America, I wanted to relax. I wanted to watch TV at night. Eventually, I convinced my mother to let me turn it on, but she always sat next to me to guard me against corruption. She would not let me watch television late at night, nor would she let me watch television by myself.

She still maintains those rules, but we do watch television every night now. Alyce and John have gotten us a cable service called "the family package." It provides only such shows as a young girl like me can watch safely. I have a few programs I watch regularly now, such as *Fear Factor*. On that show, people compete for prizes by doing unusual stunts. Yes, these include things like eating ants and snails. It does **turn your stomach**, sort of, but I enjoy it.

My mother likes to watch cooking shows—quite a change from *Fear Factor*. She also likes a channel on which they sell

....

scandalous programs filled with indecent sights unfit for the human eye shocking programs that show things that are bad or sinful

turn your stomach make you sick to watch it

clothes and other merchandise. She can follow those programs.

She also lets me watch the news now. In fact, she insists on it. She herself watches the news avidly, even if I'm not by her side. She watches for stories about our part of the world. If I'm not in the room when a segment about Afghanistan or Pakistan comes on, she yells out, "Farah! It's Kabul. Come quick! What are they saying?" We have been here for three years, but she doesn't speak much English yet, just a few scattered words. She needs me to translate everything.

All of the new clothes, pots, pans, kitchenware, phone, television, and other goods changed our life, but not nearly as much as Alyce herself. She said she would come once a week, but she started coming much more often. In fact, before long she was coming to see me every day.

With most people, I have never been much of a talker. Conversation does not come easily to me. In a group I often feel shy and keep my thoughts to myself. But Alyce brought the stories, questions, and **confidences** pouring out of me! As soon as she walked into our house, her eyes had such a sparkle and her face **wore such a flock of smiles** that my heart opened wide. When she asked me "Where do you come from?" I wanted to tell her the whole history of my life. Even that first time, after she left, I was tingling with excitement. I said to myself, *I can't be shy with this one. I have to open up and give her a chance to know who I am. She will be my friend **to the end**.*

Once we started spending time together, my English improved rapidly. We talked about every subject, so I learned

....

confidences secrets
wore such a flock of smiles was so friendly
to the end *always, forever*

the words I needed for all those different subjects. My vocabulary grew like weeds in a garden. Alyce let me ask questions of any kind and follow my curiosity wherever it led. She taught me how to become an American by telling me about the culture and customs here—what the holidays are, for example, and how you celebrate each one. She told me how to behave in a restaurant. I learned that your napkin should go on your lap. I didn't know that before.

She taught me that when you go to a wedding, you don't bring something to the party. The bride goes to a local store beforehand and gives them a list of what she wants for her house. As a guest, you are supposed to go there and buy an item from the wish list. The store keeps track of what has been bought, and thus the bride and groom get just the wares they want **with no duplicates**. It is so well organized!

Alyce told me about dating and how people don't **consider it a scandal** here when two people go out together. It's kind of normal. She said that if a young man and a young woman go out alone without their parents or an older relative along to keep watch, it's not that big of a deal. In fact, this is how people are supposed to meet in America, I discovered.

I asked Alyce how she and her husband met and how he **proposed**, and she told me the whole story. They met in college, it turned out. One of Alyce's friends knew John, and this friend said to Alyce one day, "How about going out for a drink with me tonight? I know a couple of boys who will join us." John was one of those boys. That was how he and Alyce

....

with no duplicates and no one buys the same thing
consider it a scandal think it is wrong
proposed asked her to marry him

met, and then later they started going on dates alone, just the two of them.

Eventually, he asked her to have dinner in a restaurant with him, and she suspected he was planning to propose to her that night. But John is a shy man. That night he was quieter than usual, because he was nervous about the question **on his mind**. He didn't say much as they ate their meal. After the food was gone, they just sat there and talked about **this and that little thing**, but he did not ask the big question. Finally, four hours had passed. Alyce got **exasperated**. She said, "I'm tired, and I want to go home. If you want to say something to me, say it now!"

And that's when he finally blurted out, "Will you marry me?" That's how it happened. They were engaged for a year, and then finally they got married.

Alyce invited us to her house for Thanksgiving that first year. We had never seen a turkey before and didn't know what it was. We never imagined a bird could grow so big. My mother didn't eat any of it. She knew it wasn't a pig because she saw that it had wings, but she suspected—correctly—that it had not been slaughtered in accordance with the ritual requirements of Islam, so it wasn't *halal*. She ate the potatoes and the vegetables, though, and she enjoyed those. In any case, I learned all about Thanksgiving from Alyce, and I learned the words that go with that holiday.

When you are trying to master a new language, you learn quicker if you have a chance to speak without hesitation or

....

on his mind he was thinking about
this and that little thing small things
exasperated annoyed; tired of waiting

fear. In class I didn't have the chance to speak much. I had to spend most of my time listening to the teacher. When I was called upon to say something, it was a public situation and a performance: People were looking at me, and even as I tried to **shape a thought**, I worried that I might make a mistake and that the class might laugh at me. At the same time I knew the teacher was waiting to correct me. It's easier to make progress in a language by talking with a friend and just trying to express the things you really want to say as best you can. My English improved more in a couple of weeks of chatting with Alyce than it had in three months of taking that course.

But I don't want to make it seem as if Alyce just helped me with English. As soon as she saw how much we needed, she **took it upon herself** to save our lives, and I do not use the word "save" lightly.

She saw what difficulty we had just getting food, so she began bringing groceries over to our house, or she took me to the store to buy a whole bunch of groceries at once and get them back to our apartment in a car.

When she saw that my mother needed medical care, she took it upon herself to set up her appointments and get her to the doctors on time. Alyce **set us free from those seedy**, chain-smoking, hard-drinking taxi drivers. She also went to our appointments with us. She asked the doctors the questions we didn't know how to ask. In fact, she asked the questions we didn't even know we should ask. Alyce got us better medical care because without her, the doctors could not get much

....

shape a thought think about what to say

took it upon herself kindly decided

set us free from those seedy helped us so we did not have to ride with those dishonest

information from us. They had to rely purely on what they could learn from their instruments.

In those days my mother was still having frequent asthma attacks. I had to rush her to the hospital at all odd hours. Alyce **never failed us** in those moments. I could call her at midnight, at two o'clock A.M., or at any time of night, and she would come.

I was still walking around on the prosthesis I got in Germany. It was over five years old now and really starting to fall apart, but I didn't know how to get a new one. Zainab had set up that appointment with the prosthetics lab for me when I was still her client—the one I missed because of the taxi driver. She went ahead and arranged another appointment for me and sent a taxi again, just out of the goodness of her heart. I made it to the second appointment on time, only to be told that public aid would not pay for a new prosthetic leg for me. So that **came to nothing**.

Alyce saw me hobbling about on that outsized wooden foot from the Pakistani shop, and she decided to take action. She found both a place that would make me a good prosthetic and a way to pay for it, and she took me there. By the end of the first year I had a new prosthetic leg with a foot proportional to my size. In short, I saw that Alyce was working just as hard on our behalf as we ourselves. That's when I said to myself, *At last I have someone.* I don't know what would have happened to us if Alyce had not found us.

Before I met Alyce and John, my mother and I were **living in a prison constructed of our ignorance**. Alyce opened the

....

never failed us was always there
came to nothing did not work
living in a prison constructed of our ignorance living an unhappy life because we knew so little

bars of that prison by showing us the world we now lived in. One time they took us to Holland, Michigan, for an event called the Tulip Festival. We strolled through the most beautiful set of gardens I have ever seen. It reminded me of a scene in a famous Bollywood movie in which a girl sings a song in a tulip field. At the Holland Tulip Festival, I felt like that girl.

Another time Alyce and John took me into the city of Chicago to a place called the Field Museum. There, I saw things that opened my eyes—wonderful things! The whole experience took me back to the way I had felt in second grade, listening to our beloved teacher, Ma'lim Sahib, talking about the stars. I felt like I was finally **picking up the thread the land mine broke**. The museum was saying to me, *Here is the world again, and look how big it is and how much it contains!*

I saw stuffed animals there, from all parts of the world. I learned what sorts of creatures live in the jungles and deserts, and on the slopes of high mountains, and in the deepest oceans, all without having to go to those difficult environments.

The Field Museum had mummies, too. I had never heard of mummies before. I never dreamed that such a thing as a mummy could exist in our world, yet here they were, along with pictures of Egypt, the country where they came from. The museum had pictures of the pyramids and temples and monuments that the people of Egypt built in ancient times. You could get an idea of what life was like back then, and what people believed, and why and how they turned their kings and other famous dead people into mummies. In second grade

....

picking up the thread the land mine broke enjoying learning again, like I did before I stepped on the land mine

I marveled to learn merely that other countries existed, countries where people rode trains and went about bareheaded and spoke languages unlike mine. Now I discovered that the world **was even more inconceivably various** than I had imagined back then.

At this museum they had room-size boxes showing scenes of everyday life as it existed in this very area, less than two hundred years ago. They showed how the native people lived at that time—in houses made of animal skins, wearing clothing made of fur, using tools made of reeds and bones . . . The scenes showed how they hunted animals with bows and arrows and traveled from place to place on rivers in handmade canoes of tree bark. They showed everything.

These boxed scenes were like moments of real life, frozen in time, complete with realistic figures of the people themselves wearing the actual clothes of their culture and handling the actual goods and tools they made—the canoes, the bows, the hatchets. It was so interesting to look into those boxes and realize that people followed this way of life not so very long ago, right where this museum now stood. And these were Americans. In fact, these were the real and original Americans—and yet they were so undeveloped, even compared to Afghans. They did not know about science and machinery and modern technology until the British came. It made me ponder why some ways of life succeed and spread while others succumb to time and vanish. It made me think about the differences that exist today between America and Afghanistan

....

was even more inconceivably various was filled with even more things and why my homeland is **mired in such difficulties** and why it can't seem to shake its way out of its problems.

I also saw dinosaurs at this museum. I had never heard of dinosaurs before I came to America. Now I saw the skeletons of these monsters and models of what they looked like. I saw a film about the people who find dinosaur bones. They work so carefully, it amazes you! When they find something in the ground that might be a bone, they rub it with a delicate brush so it won't shatter or break. This work really caught my interest.

A few days after that visit to the museum I saw a show about dinosaurs on television. I watched it with Alyce. That night when I went to sleep, I saw a dinosaur in my dreams. It was running through a jungle, and I was in that jungle, too. In fact, the dinosaur was chasing me. I was running as hard as I could, and I turned my head to see if it was **gaining**, and at that very moment it took off in one tremendous bounding leap that lifted it into the air and brought it arcing toward me. The sun vanished in its shadow, and its shadow grew around me as it descended, down and down until—*whump!* The **impact** of its body on mine woke me up.

Yes, I woke up with a jolt, because my teddy bear had fallen off a shelf, onto my neck. But in the grogginess of that moment I still thought it was the dinosaur, and I tangled with it. We wrestled. I managed to fling it away in total horror, hard enough that it hit the wall with a thud. The next morning I picked up the poor teddy bear and apologized.

So dinosaurs got mixed into my nightmares, but outside

....

mired in such difficulties unable to overcome its problems
gaining catching up to me
impact hit

of the nightmares, I found them fascinating creatures—why were they so different from the animals we see today? Their size! Their shapes! And how interesting that we don't see such creatures anymore. They populated Earth in huge numbers at one time and nothing could **stand up to** them, and now they are all gone. That is so strange. It makes you think about the world and what lasts and what doesn't.

Another time Alyce and John took me sailing on Lake Michigan. John's brother has a sailboat, so we went for a ride one summer afternoon. They gave me some medicine before we started, which was supposed to stop a person from getting sick. I never really felt sick, and I rode that boat without any fear, even though we sailed until we could no longer see land in any direction. The wind drove the boat along, so we never went very fast, but the boat moved up and down and back and forth in a sort of constant rolling motion that made me dizzy, especially if I stood at the rails and looked out. They tried to **distract me from the motion** by giving me food. They gave me lots and lots of food, but it didn't help. I found the whole experience pretty interesting at the time, but later I realized it exhausted me, because as soon as we got home, I fell asleep, and I more or less slept for two days. I didn't throw up, so I guess the tablet worked, but I never went sailing again. Two days of recovery from one day of sailing doesn't seem like a worthwhile trade.

I am very fond of Alyce's husband, John. He is such a gentleman, so smart and hardworking. He and I have spent a lot of time together. He took me to summer school every day

----

stand up to defeat, stop

distract me from the motion keep me from thinking about my dizziness one summer. We have talked about many things while driving. John is a businessman. He shares his business experiences with me, which I like, because maybe I will run a business one day myself. Whenever he goes on a business trip, he tells me all about it when he comes back, and I like to hear his stories.

John took me to a golf course a few times. He loves golf, and he wanted to teach me how to play the game. I didn't know what I was doing, but he said, "You're doing good. Now you're getting it, excellent, excellent!" In fact, I did manage to hit the ball, and it went way up high.

He took me to play Ping-Pong one time, too, and it was fun, but mostly because of John.

Alyce and John have a daughter, and she's nice, too. I don't know her very well, because she is grown up and lives **on her own**, but I can tell that she's nice because she's never jealous of all the attention Alyce gives me. If my mom were to give this much attention to someone else, I would go crazy. So I admire Alyce's daughter for sharing her mother with me like this.

I am a strong person. I have **drive**, and I want to study, but without Alyce and John, I might have given up, because I had no supporters, no encouragement. Alyce and John Litz **restored my zest for life** by giving me love, by **pampering** me, by giving me their attention. They give me a kind of attention I didn't even get from my own family, not even when we were all alive and together.

To be honest, I'm a little spoiled now. These people praise me when I do well at something, but they give me positive

....

on her own by herself

drive goals, ambition

restored my zest for life helped me love life again

pampering being very nice to

attention even when I don't do so well. I draw a picture and I can see that it isn't great—I have eyes—but they still say, "What a lovely artist you are! What a talent you have." They tell me I'm pretty. They tell me I'm cute. They call me "honey" and "sweetie." They give me energy and life and hope. I love them so much. One day, if God wills it, I will be a strong, successful adult, and I will be there for them when they are old and need love, care, and attention. **May Allah will that I** have a chance to give them as much as they have given me.

When I was little, I was part of a big family in which everyone cared about everyone—but no one paid that much attention to me in particular. Frankly, it isn't the custom in Afghanistan for adults to give a lot of individual attention to any one child. On top of that, I was one of five children in my family, and on top of that, there were many other children around, too, the children of my aunts and uncles, and then I was so young when I stepped on that land mine and **got snatched out of** my family and world, and then I lost my family and had to go to Pakistan—so I never got much love or attention growing up. I had a sad and serious childhood. In fact, I barely had a childhood at all. I was forced to grow up very suddenly. Alyce and John are letting me live a little of my childhood now, even though I am **past the time** for it. They let me behave in very childish ways sometimes—I make demands and act silly. Better late than never. When I'm with those two, I don't even think of myself as a young woman. I don't think about the fact that I am grown up and should act my age. Instead, I say, "Take

....

May Allah will that I I hope that God lets me
got snatched out of suddenly had to leave
past the time too old

me out! I want ice cream!"

But then I think about how much they have done for me, God love them, and I think **I should hold back**. As they say in Afghanistan, when someone extends their hand, don't climb on their shoulder. But I couldn't help it. When Alyce met me, I was like a drowning girl. She reached out her hand, and I started climbing up her arm. I know I should watch myself and hold back, and yet I act like a child with them.

On the other hand, in many ways, I am older than most kids my age. I have a serious side—too serious, probably. It's as if there are pools of darkness in me. One thing I love about Alyce is that she can accept me in my dark moods. Some days the pressure comes upon me and the world **grows stormy**. My past rises inside me, and I remember things that make me angry, or I grow lonely or sullen or sad, or I brim with unbearable feelings that I cannot name or express. Alyce accepts anything that comes out of me in these moods. She doesn't turn against me when I snap or rage at her—and I do, believe me, sometimes it gets pretty rough. She just listens quietly and lets me rant till I am spent and can rage no more. Then she gives me a hug and says, "Oh, I am so sorry."

How could I not love a person like that?

Even though we grew up so differently, we have things in common. Her mother, too, had emotional problems. Alyce was the youngest of three siblings, and she grew up feeling unnoticed. She had a lonely childhood, and so she understands about loneliness. She says, "That's why I gave my own daughter

....

I should hold back I should not ask for so much

grows stormy becomes difficult

so much attention. That's why I give you so much attention. Believe me, I understand about loneliness."

One day Alyce told me a story. She said that just before September 11 she was reading a book called *The Princess*. It told about the way women lived in countries like Saudi Arabia. Then she read another book called *Stolen Lives*, which also told about the situation of women in places like Afghanistan under the Taliban.

These books **stirred her heart**, and she wanted to connect with someone from that part of the world, so she began exploring how to start **a correspondence with** a Muslim woman. She wanted to find a **pen pal**, but then 9/11 happened, and suddenly it was much harder for an American woman to make a connection with a Muslim woman, much harder for any two people in these two worlds to get to know each other.

Alyce told me she prayed that God would somehow give her a pen pal. Now, she said, she believed that God had answered her prayer more fully than she had imagined possible. Instead of a pen pal, she had gotten a real live human being, someone she could get to know in real life—she got me.

Then I told her about my experience in Quetta, when I **relinquished** myself to Allah and felt that he had taken notice of me and had a plan for me. Alyce is such an important part of my story. I don't know if God sent us to each other, but I know God gave her that big heart, which she shares with me. Of course, she has helped a lot of people in need. She works with a nonprofit organization called LOVE Christian Clearinghouse.

....

stirred her heart filled her with emotion
a correspondence with writing to
pen pal person to write to regularly
relinquished gave

She is the president of the board of directors of this group, which partners with ninety-four churches in this area. She has organized volunteers to help many refugees and other poor and needy people, and she has given her own time to many people before me. But with me, I think there is something more. Alyce and I have a special connection, and she says so, too. I think this connection comes from God.

When we came to America, my mother was thinking, *What if my daughter loses her religion and becomes a Christian here?* When I discarded my head scarf, she panicked. In those early days, when I went out with Alyce, she stayed awake watching for me. She worried that this woman would take me to church and force me to **convert**, or that she would take me to unsuitable movies, to dances and parties—that she would corrupt me.

But Alyce was simply **nourishing my spirit**. She was the one person who took an interest in any progress I made, the one person to whom I could recount my day's adventures. Everyone needs an audience of at least one.

John and Alyce never say, *Oh, you should eat pork* or *A little wine won't harm you* or *Don't listen to your mom.* In fact, when we go to a restaurant, Alyce reads the menu carefully to make sure there's no pork or alcohol in any of the dishes. They never say, *Your religion is no good, our religion is better, you should come over to our religion.*

When my mother and I go to her house, Alyce lets my mother know when it is prayer time, which room she can pray in, and even which way she should turn to **face Mecca**. Alyce is

----

convert change religions
nourishing my spirit making me feel loved
face Mecca pray toward the Muslim holy city

so thoughtful that way. And she cooks with *halal* meat for us, so that my mother will be able to eat.

Alyce does ask about my religion, and she listens to what I say and tries to understand. I am no scholar, but I tell her what I know about Islam. I tell her we believe that God-dear is unique and one-of-a-kind, a light that one sees with one's heart, not with one's eyes. I tell her, "We respect and love Jesus, too. He is one of our **prophets**. We know his **stature** and believe he will return to **herald** the Day of Judgment." She listens without interrupting.

Then she tells me what she believes, and I listen. I see nothing wrong with listening to each other's beliefs. I want to know about her religion, just as she wants to know about mine. We can talk about our beliefs without pushing each other to feel wrong. This is one reason why I love her so much.

But there are many other reasons that I love her, too. She's funny. She makes me laugh. When I'm with her, I forget my problems. I don't think of her as an American or a foreigner or this or that nationality. **It never crosses my mind** that she's an adult woman, so much older than me. Different ages, different religions, different nationalities—none of that matters. She's my friend. It's as simple as that. She calls me at least once a day, and we talk about everything. With her, whatever comes into my heart comes out of my mouth. We hide nothing from each other.

....

prophets religious leaders

stature important position

herald announce

It never crosses my mind I never think

BEFORE YOU MOVE ON...

1. **Summarize** Farah calls Alyce Litz an "angel." What did Alyce do to help Farah?

2. **Paraphrase** Reread page 232. Farah writes, "Alyce and John are letting me live a little of my childhood now." What does she mean?

LOOK AHEAD Read to page 250 to find out how Farah adjusts to school in America.

HIGH SCHOOL IN AMERICA

⸻❧⸻

As I said, I wanted to start school as soon as **my feet hit American soil**, but we arrived too late in the year. Summer vacation was about to start, so I had to wait until the following September. When the time came at last, Alyce figured out which district I lived in and which school I was supposed to attend. She also found out when I should register.

We refugees were supposed to start a week later than the others, for some reason. The day I arrived on campus, the regular students had already started classes. I saw them all over the yard and in the halls and classrooms, hundreds upon hundreds of American kids! **My heart quailed.**

After I completed my paperwork in the office, they sent me to another room to meet with my counselor and work out my

....

my feet hit American soil I arrived in the U.S.
My heart quailed. I was afraid and worried.

schedule. On the way I saw more American students swarming up and down the stairs, laughing and talking together in groups, throwing their arms around one another. I felt like I ought to be one of them, because I was about the same age, and yet I felt so separate, so different. Some of them were clad in black clothes from head to foot and wore heavy chains around their necks. I had no idea what their uniforms **signified**. All the students intimidated me, but those especially.

My counselor discussed what classes I should take and then told me I would start the following week. When I got home, I said, "W'Allah! How will I do, going to school with so many Americans? Will they stare? Will they laugh at me? If try to talk to them, I will probably say the wrong thing. Will they tease me?" Each night that week, as I tried to get to sleep, I pictured myself surrounded by jeering American kids asking why I walked like I did and what was wrong with my leg. I pictured them cursing me and hitting me.

Finally, the big day came, and I went to school. I was entering as a freshman. As it turned out, all my classmates that year were going to be ESL students. They came from Mexico, from Spain, from India, from Russia—from many countries. I had no American classmates that year at all. But Americans surrounded me in the hallways as I moved from one class to another, and they surrounded me in the lunchroom.

To my surprise, however, none of them even glanced at me, much less spoke to me. They just **went by in a blur**. I began to cheer up and believe I might survive at this school. I saw that

....

signified meant
went by in a blur passed by me

my fellow students were not going to tease me, because I wasn't even **in the world of their concerns**. They didn't notice that I even existed. Later I began to want more attention, but in those early days **invisibility suited me just fine**. I felt relieved.

During that first week a teacher's aide went everywhere with me. She showed me all the places I needed to know about in that school: my classrooms, the cafeteria, the locker area, and so on. I needed that guidance because it was a big three-story building, and I could easily have gotten lost. My English classes were on the third floor, my math class on the second floor, and my art class on the first floor.

In my ESL classes I got to know an Indian girl named Apanza. I met two Afghan girls as well. They had come to America one year earlier than I and had therefore gone to American schools one year longer, but we were all in the same class. In any case, I had companions now. I could speak with the Afghan girls in Farsi and with the Indian girl in Urdu, which I had learned in Pakistan. At lunchtime my new friends and I always ate together in the school cafeteria. After a while I stopped feeling quite so lonely.

My favorite classes were English and art. I liked art because I didn't have to listen or speak there. I could just draw or paint, which I found blessedly restful. After Christmas I signed up for a piano class, too. I had never seen a piano before, but I learned to play the instrument a bit, although I've forgotten everything I learned by now. At the end of the semester, however, I **took part in my class's recital**. A few weeks before the show the

....

in the world of their concerns part of their thoughts
invisibility suited me just fine I liked not being noticed
took part in my class's recital played in front of an audience
with my class

teacher presented each of us with a list of tunes and asked us to pick one. I chose a song called "Money Can't Buy You Love." I practiced it every day and then played it at the recital. All the parents came to watch the performance. My mother was there, and so was my "other mother," Alyce. The Indian girl's parents came, too. I made a few mistakes, but it didn't matter. The parents all enjoyed the show. They would have clapped no matter how or what we played.

I found math especially difficult. I had studied math **formally** only to the second grade, and that was in Afghanistan, where we went to school only a couple of hours a day. All I learned there were the small numbers. In school I never learned the big numbers. Later, in Pakistan, somehow or other, I learned to add, subtract, and even divide a little, just from handling money. Along the way I picked up a few of the multiplication tables, too—maybe half of them. When I was tested for basic math skills and they gave me problems that involved adding or subtracting, I could do them. I could do division problems, too, but only with small, even numbers. If three- or four-digit numbers were involved, I got lost. And if a subtraction problem involved borrowing, I couldn't do that, either. They put me in basic math that first year, but since I **progressed quickly**, they decided to **bump me ahead** to pre-algebra toward the end of the year.

There, I didn't do so well, in part because I couldn't follow the teacher's English. And since I couldn't learn anything from his explanations, I had to watch what he wrote on the

....

formally in school
progressed quickly learned fast
bump me ahead let me study

chalkboard and try to figure out what he might be saying. The math had gotten ahead of my English. I wanted to **drop back**, but the counselor told me, "No, stick with what you're doing. You'll catch up eventually."

As soon as the regular school year ended, I started summer school because I could not afford to take any time off. I studied English from eight a.m. to noon, and then from twelve thirty to four, I took Algebra I. I should have taken a pre-algebra class in summer school, but they didn't offer it, so I **jumped into** the only math class they did offer.

In that class I **floundered**. All the other students were American kids who had failed Algebra I during the school year and were taking it again to get credit. The teacher assumed that all of us were going through this material for the second time, so he moved very fast. As soon as I discovered how hard it was, I wanted to drop out, but Alyce encouraged me to stay in the course. "It's free," she pointed out. "You're sure to learn *something*," And she added, "It's okay to fail, you know."

Well, I stayed in the course, but I didn't feel like it was okay to fail. That's just not **my temperament**. So I tried very hard to catch up, but I just couldn't, and the effort brought me to tears.

Alyce saw me in that state one day and said, "Come home with me. Let's have some tea and talk it over." When we got to her house, she said, "What you really need is a little fun. We can talk about algebra later." Alyce had a bride's outfit at home, a white dress with a beautiful gauzy veil and some flowers. She got me to dress up in that outfit and took pictures of me.

....

drop back return to an easier class
jumped into joined, took
floundered could not keep up; struggled
my temperament the kind of person I am

Alyce knew I liked being photographed, and it was great fun pretending to get married. And forgetting about algebra for a few hours did make me feel a bit better.

But it did nothing to improve my algebra. I did fail that course. And yet Alyce was right: Somehow I did learn something. When school started back up, I decided to take basic math again, in order to **get a really solid foundation in** math. I learned fractions, multiplication, long division—everything you're supposed to learn in your first seven years of math, and I got an A. Now I'm taking pre-algebra again, and I'm understanding it finally. I'm getting a B. I'm catching up. **Phew!**

My ESL classes in my sophomore year were two hours long—two hours in a row of nothing but English. I had to put everything else out of my mind and focus entirely on the teacher, never missing a word. I knew I had to master the language before I could succeed at anything else in this country, but when you focus really hard like that, when you **cling so tightly to the thread of one person's voice**, you can't lose hold of the thread for an instant. If you do—and it's inevitable that you will for an instant or two sometime in the course of two hours—you shoot instantly into another universe as if shot from a bow. That kept happening to me in ESL class. One moment I would be listening to the teacher, and the next moment I would find myself deep in my past, wrestling with my demons, drowning in panic. And I would have to shake my head to wake out of it and tell myself, *No, no, Farah! You're in America now. Pay attention to the teacher, the teacher.*

....

get a really solid foundation in really learn

Phew! What a relief!

cling so tightly to the thread of one person's voice listen closely to every word a person is saying

After concentrating so hard, I often left school feeling dizzy. My head usually hurt. I took the school bus home, and it always rocked with the commotion, noise, and **hullabaloo** of the other students. One day I decided to shut my eyes and **seek silence in the privacy of my own mind**. But I must have fallen asleep. When I opened my eyes, I saw that we had come to a stop someplace I had never seen before. The bus was empty, and the bus driver was shouting, "Get off! Get off!"

I said, "I missed my stop. Could you take me back to school or back to my bus stop or back to any place I've ever seen before?"

She said, "No! This is the **end of the line, and my shift is over**. Get down here and go! Wherever your house is, go there now. You're on your own."

So I got out and started walking back the way we had come. How many blocks I walked, I don't know. I just walked and walked, that's all I know. My poor mother was sitting at home, chewing on her fingernails and looking at the clock, thinking, *Where is that girl? Has she been kidnapped?* If I was late, that's the conclusion she always jumped to: The girl has been kidnapped.

My English was not very good yet, and strangers scared me, so I didn't want to ask for directions. I just kept going until I reached an area I recognized, but I found myself on the wrong side of an extremely busy street with no stoplights. I had to get to the other side, but it was like crossing an expressway. By the time I got home that day, I was trembling. Some days were better and some worse, but I always came home from

....

hullabaloo activity

seek silence in the privacy of my own mind sit quietly and think

end of the line, and my shift is over last bus stop and I am going home

school exhausted.

In my freshman year they put me in ESL I. After that year, in summer school, I got through ESL II. In my sophomore year I made it through ESL III. Now I'm in ESL IV. At this level only your English class is ESL. You study all the rest of your subjects with the **mainstream students**. Strangely enough, it's less demanding. In the ESL classes they give more homework. Now I can get my homework done at school.

Next year I'll be out of ESL altogether. Even my English class will be mainstream. Officially, at least, I'll be caught up. And it's true that I can speak and understand English pretty well now, but I still have trouble with reading and writing. The thing is, I am not just learning to read and write in English. I am learning to read and write **period**. I only studied to the middle of second grade, when **my life fell apart**. All I learned in Afghanistan was the alphabet, that's all. Even in my native language, I could never read a newspaper or a storybook. Once I came to America, I had to learn a new language, English, and also these new skills, reading and writing. It has been a struggle.

And spelling is difficult in its own right. I don't think people appreciate how difficult spelling in English is if you don't grow up speaking the language. In the three years that I have been going to school in America, I have not had one class that covered spelling. Actually, many of the American students seem to have problems with spelling, too. I know that they teach spelling in the lower grades here, but I think they should teach

....

mainstream students students in regular English-speaking classes

period for the first time

my life fell apart the land mine changed my life

it in high school, too, for those who need it—and many do.

I read books as much as I can, to improve my language skills. Recently, for example, I read *Of Mice and Men* by John Steinbeck. I wrote an essay about it for my final exam in English last semester. I liked that book, but it did not really touch me emotionally—not like the movie. Oh my gosh! In the movie, when the man's brother kills that little girl, I just started crying. That movie affected me powerfully. I need to improve my English to the point where a book can **get to me** that way.

One book I really liked was *Across Five Aprils*, a novel about the Civil War. And there's another book—I've forgotten the title now, but it tells the story of an African girl who was brought to America as a slave. She really, really wants to learn how to read and write. That's her main struggle. Finally, another slave on the plantation, an older man, teaches her these skills. I forget the girl's name—I'm not good with names—but this was a nonfiction biography. She was a real person. Oh my gosh, I could relate to her story! I found her life very inspiring.

As I mentioned, when I first thought about coming to America, people in Pakistan told me, "Don't go, you will become a slave there." At the time I found such tales **baffling**. Why did people make up these stories? I wondered. Where did they get ideas like this? But here in America, I learned about the Civil War. And this year, in American history class, I learned how this country was founded. I read how the European settlers fought with the Indians. I realized that there was some kernel of truth to the stories people were telling in

....

get to me affect me
baffling confusing

Pakistan. Americans did at one time import people from other continents and keep them here as slaves. The Europeans who came to this land did fight with the native people, and terrible things happened. I think people in Pakistan heard some fragments from the history of America, and they never **caught on** that these things belong to the past. I think that many people in Pakistan don't know that slavery is now against the law in America.

I learned another **astounding** fact about U.S. history from my studies. This country was built by refugees. And yet look how it has advanced, look how it has developed! The United States is much younger than Afghanistan, as it turns out—and this information surprised me. Afghanistan is very ancient. The same people have been living there for thousands of years, with one culture, one way of life, one religion—and yet, oh, how far behind they have fallen! Here, where people from many cultures, many religions, and many parts of the planet have come together, they have built such an advanced society. It amazes me.

I ask myself why this is so. *Why has America done so well?*

In our American history class I read that when people came here from so many places, they came with ambition, they came to start over, and they worked hard. That's probably part of it. Also, they were able to **raise their voices** here. They were able to express themselves and search for their own beliefs and say what they believed out loud. I think that is why America has developed so remarkably. Here, people can live their lives

....

caught on realized, learned
astounding amazing, interesting
raise their voices say what they thought

without fear. In places like Afghanistan, by contrast, everybody is afraid. Nobody dares to raise his voice. I think America has grown strong because it lets everyone **take a part**.

Over in Pakistan and Afghanistan and places like that, it isn't just the government that holds society back. People are afraid of their neighbors, of what "others will say." People **hold one another in check**. Here, you can try something new. If you invent something, people will congratulate you and take an interest in your invention. There, they will say, "Why did you invent this thing? We don't want something different! What was wrong with what we had before?" Here, you can announce your opinion, and if you're against something, you can say so and it becomes part of the discussion, not a reason why you have to go into hiding.

I don't know why such differences exist among countries, but I think it's important that in America the law says you can express yourself. I think the Bill of Rights makes the big difference. The Bill of Rights gives Americans the freedom of religion, the freedom of speech, the freedom to meet and gather and make plans.

I like studying the history of America and of the world. Even though school is a struggle, I enjoy it, and I have been making progress. Every year in my school the teachers keep track of their students on a score sheet. They grade students not just on their academic work, but also on how attentive they are, how faithfully they do their homework, how much they contribute to the positive atmosphere of the school, how well

....

take a part participate, contribute
hold one another in check stop each other from doing or saying what they want to

they behave, what **citizenship qualities** they demonstrate, and so on. At the end of each semester they add up all the numbers and whoever gets the highest score is named Outstanding Student of the Semester.

At the end of my sophomore year I won that award. My teacher told me about it in English class. Then, on a certain day, the principal, the teachers, the students, and many of the parents got together at the school for a ceremony. My mother came, too. So did Alyce and John.

The ceremony began with a nice breakfast. The principal then announced the award and called me up to the stage. I stood there while my teacher gave a speech about me. Then I got **a plaque** that read OUTSTANDING STUDENT OF 2004, SECOND SEMESTER, along with a twenty-five-dollar gift certificate to a local department store. A photographer took my picture up there with all those teachers and school officials. The picture was posted in the hall at my school. It felt good to see my picture on the wall every morning when I came to school. It made me feel known.

Now, in my junior year, I spend much of my time each day with Americans, for most of my classes are non-ESL. And yet, even though I am **"on Main Street"** now, I don't interact with American students all that much. We're friendly enough at school, but after school they go their way and I go mine.

We ESL students have to work longer hours than other students. Some of us have jobs, but even those who don't work for money have to spend a lot of time studying and doing

....

citizenship qualities good behavior

a plaque an award

"on Main Street" with the rest of the English-speaking students

homework because we have so much catching up to do. We would like to take part in clubs and after-school activities with American kids, and go to the movies with them sometimes, and listen to CDs and find out what kind of music people like here. We would like to go out with kids our age and talk and joke and tell stories and have fun, but many of us don't have time.

But our struggle is not the whole story. The American kids **hold themselves apart, too**. They don't mingle or form friendships with kids from other countries. Whatever they do socially—and I don't know what that is—they do it among themselves. I have no American friends my age.

I guess it's partly because the American kids grew up here and found their friends long ago. They don't need more friends now, so they ignore anyone they don't already know. If you say hi, they say hi back, but it doesn't lead to conversation.

I wonder, though, if my American classmates are also intimidated by us. Maybe we embarrass them or something like that. Anyway, something holds them back. Certainly, we refugee kids are afraid of them. We're also ashamed of our situation—of being so **dependent, impoverished, and out of place**. That's what holds us back from making friends. We feel shame. I know that many refugees feel this way. We're ashamed that we don't know English very well. It's hard for us to start conversations. We don't want to take the first step because we assume we'll be rejected. We think, *Why should an American kid, who has everything, want to waste his or her time with a poor refugee?*

....

hold themselves apart, too do not offer their friendship either

dependant, impoverished, and out of place needy, poor, and unable to fit in

I know it's hard for American students to reach out to us refugees, and maybe you worry about being rejected or **put on the spot**. But here is one thing I want to say in this book: It's harder for us to reach out to you—we, with our clumsy English. I want to say, Don't be afraid of us—you have to understand: *We're* afraid of *you*. We want to make friends, but you have to take the first step.

And there's another thing for us refugees: Our English can't improve if we never use it in ordinary daily life. We can't **get up to speed** just by taking classes. We need to have friendships and to hang around with you Americans and talk easily back and forth. Otherwise, when we leave school, we just go to our homes. Where else can we go? And at home everyone speaks our home language. We study our books, but it's not the same as having friends. We want to join American culture, but American culture has to let us in. It's hard for us to get aggressive and push our way in. It's easier for us if we feel invited. That's what you can do. Invite us in. Everyday friendships with Americans would **alleviate our longing for our homelands**. We would feel ourselves to be a part of this world. We would enjoy going to school, and we would lose our homesickness.

That's what I want to say. We're shy. You have to start first.

....

put on the spot feeling embarrassed

get up to speed learn well or quickly

alleviate our longing for our homelands help us stop missing our home countries

BEFORE YOU MOVE ON...

1. **Conclusions** Reread page 244. Why was school so hard for Farah during the first two years?

2. **Author's Point of View** Reread pages 246–247. Why does Farah think America has "done so well"?

LOOK AHEAD Read pages 251–260 to find out why Farah has problems learning to drive.

LEARNING TO DRIVE

About a year and a half after I arrived in America, Alyce and I went to a prosthetics clinic in downtown Chicago to **look into** getting a new leg for me. A lady came out of the clinic as we were heading toward the door. This woman had a prosthetic leg. If you yourself have a prosthesis, you can always tell when someone else has one. I noticed this woman as soon as she came out of the building. I watched her go to one of the cars in the parking lot. I assumed that she was going to go to the passenger's side, and I wondered where her driver might be. Instead, to my surprise, she opened the door on the driver's side. I said, "**Whoa!** Is she going to drive that thing?" I slowed down to watch, and indeed that is just what she did do. She got in, shut the door, turned on the engine, and zoom– she went

----

look into find out about
Whoa! Oh no!

driving off!

I nudged Alyce. "Did you see that woman? She had a prosthesis, yet she drove that car!"

Alyce said, "Well! If she can do it, so can you. Right, Farah?"

The idea that I might one day drive a car **thrilled me to the core**. It felt like a window had opened and given me a glimpse of a whole new lifetime of possibilities.

I decided to take driver's education at school the next semester—they call it "driver's ed." In that class I learned the rules of the road—for example, about stop signs and turn signals and what my rights were and what other people's rights were. I learned what to do if I got in a car accident—how I shouldn't drive away, but stop and trade information with the other driver; how we should both wait for the police. I learned what to do if I had a flat tire.

The only thing I didn't learn in driver's ed was how to drive. They couldn't teach me that, because they didn't have any cars **specially fitted out** for disabled people.

I was so disappointed. I **collared** Alyce and said, "Please, please, make it happen. I want to learn to drive. I'll do anything. How can I do this?"

So Alyce, poor thing, did some research. She found a place in Wheaton called the Marianjoy Rehab Hospital, which had a special program that helped people like me learn to drive. They charged money, however, and I could not afford their services. So Alyce talked to administrators at my high school. She said, "You're supposed to offer driver's education to all your students.

....

thrilled me to the core made me very happy
specially fitted out with special controls
collared grabbed

Since you're not **equipped** to offer it to this girl, it seems only right that you pay for her to take driving lessons at Marianjoy, where they do have the necessary equipment."

Amazingly enough, the school agreed.

One week after I started driver's ed at school, I went to Marianjoy with Alyce. It was a one-story building, and we had to step around a lot of construction because they were tearing down one building and putting up another, but we got inside finally, and Alyce told the receptionist, "This girl has an appointment."

The teacher came out to meet us, a young woman. She started by putting me through a series of tests. For example, she gave me a sort of vision test. She showed me a shape on a piece of paper. Then she turned the paper over. On the other side were five more shapes. One of them, she said, was the same shape I had just seen, but from a different angle. She wanted me to pick out which one.

I passed that test and all the other tests the teacher gave me. She then took me to a car **outfitted** with hand controls. One lever was for shifting gears. Another was both brake and accelerator in one. You turned it one way to make the car go and the other way to make the car stop. We got into the car, and I started driving. At least, I tried to follow the teacher's instructions, but I couldn't do it. I just could not **sort out** turning from accelerating to braking to shifting gears. The car went all over the place. I drove onto the lawn. I drove into the bushes. Luckily, my teacher was sitting right next to me with

....

equipped able
outfitted built, designed
sort out understand

controls of her own that **overrode mine**. She kept me from crashing into people and buildings. But I drove **this way and that** on their special roads, going too fast or going too slow, and always, always, going in the wrong direction.

I came home, and my shoulders hurt for three days because I had been so tense. I lost hope. I said, "Driving is too hard. I can't do it."

But time passed, and I began to think about my problem. I watched what Alyce did when she drove. One day I told Alyce, "Look. It's true that I cannot bend my right leg at the knee, but I can still bend my foot. And this other leg is a prosthesis, but I can push with it, and I can bend the knee, too. Why don't I try driving a regular car?" This was my own idea. "Let me just try it," I said.

We went back to Marianjoy. Alyce explained my idea to those people. The teacher tried to talk me out of driving a regular car. She said, "Be patient. You'll **get the hang of hand controls by and by**. Give it time."

I said, "No, I think I can drive a regular car. Let me just try it."

So the teacher took me into a special room and tested my reactions and leg strength. In one test, for example, I was supposed to press a pedal each time a light flashed.

Well, I passed all these tests, proving that I could do everything a driver needed to do with her feet. Finally, the teacher said, "Well . . . okay. Let's try it with an actual car." But she said this in a dubious voice. She still didn't favor the idea.

....

overrode mine stopped my controls

this way and that everywhere

get the hang of hand controls by and by learn how to drive using your hands soon

We got into a regular car, and I discovered a new problem. I was too short. I could not reach the gas pedal with my foot no matter how far forward I pushed my chair.

The teacher said, "Well, there's a place that adapts cars to the needs of people with disabilities. They make hand controls, lifts, and all sorts of other devices. Why don't you go see if they have anything that might help you?"

The place was very far away, but Alyce said, "No problem." We drove out there the next day. The mechanic at this workshop was a warm and friendly man. He said, "Yes, actually, we do make a platform that mounts to a gas pedal and **builds it up**." In fact, he made two different kinds of platforms. He gave us one and told us to try it. He said that if it didn't work, we should bring it back and try the other model.

We took the platform to Marianjoy, **clamped** it to the gas pedal of one of their cars, and it worked perfectly! Now, at last, I could actually start learning to drive, and it was *easy*. I couldn't believe how easy driving turned out to be! Once a week that semester, I went in for a one-hour lesson, and I progressed quickly from Marianjoy's special lot to the street, to bigger streets, to driving in traffic. It just went so smoothly.

In fact, the driver's ed class at school was harder than driving itself. There, in driver's ed, they did their best to scare you. They showed films of people who had been injured or killed in car accidents. Every week they showed videos of horrible crashes and **mangled** people. They explained how and why each crash happened, all to warn us about the dangers

....

builds it up adds height to it
clamped fastened, attached
mangled badly injured

of speeding and especially about the dangers of driving after drinking alcohol. They brought in people who had been injured in accidents caused by drunk drivers, to tell us their stories. They also brought in people who had gotten drunk and caused accidents that hurt or killed people. Talking to classes like ours was part of these people's punishment. No matter who came in, they showed images of dead or wounded people. We all left that class **panting with fear**.

For me, those videos of car crashes and those images of blood and mangled flesh were hard to tolerate. Instead of teaching me anything about driving, they **put me back in** that hospital in Kabul, with all the injured children, one of whom was me. Nowadays I can look at images of bloodshed a bit more easily than I could then. I still don't like it, but I don't get quite so upset; but in those days—phew! I could hardly bear it!

According to the rules, after I got my learner's permit, I had to practice driving with someone else in the car for at least twenty-five hours before I could take my driving test. It was John who took me out after work and on weekends to complete those many hours of practice. He was so patient with me and so wonderfully calm. It was John who really taught me to drive. Even when I did something wrong, he would say, "Never mind. Don't worry. Try again. You can do it."

One girl I knew at school (and I won't mention her name) always tried to make me feel handicapped and unworthy. For some reason, making me feel smaller made her feel bigger. I don't understand why, but when I mentioned that I was learning

....

panting with fear very afraid
put me back in made me remember

to drive, she jeered at me. She said they would never give a driver's license to someone like me. "Even I flunked the driver's test the first time I took it," she said. "How could you possibly expect to pass?"

Even so, one day I told Alyce, "I want to take the test this week."

Alyce said, "Oh, Farah—are you *suuuure*?"

I said, "Yes! I'm ready." And I was. Parallel parking, uphill, downhill—I did it all! I passed my driving test the very first time I took it and came home with my license. When I showed it to the girl who said I could never do it, she frowned and **got all sulky.**

Of course, a driver's license didn't do me much good without a car, but once again, dear Alyce came to the rescue. She phoned around to all the organizations she knew about, all the churches, all her friends. Alyce knows a lot of people from her work with LOVE Christian Clearinghouse. She asked everyone she knew to ask everyone *they* knew if *anyone* had a car they might want to **donate** to me.

Someone suggested that she contact a man named Chris Gossett. She called this fellow and explained the situation, and he wanted to help. During the conversation he revealed that he was a dentist by profession, but **as a side business and hobby,** he bought old cars, fixed them up, and sold them. He didn't have a suitable car at that moment, he said, but he would keep an eye out for one. In the meantime, he offered to look at my teeth. Dr. Gossett is a really nice, gentle man.

....

got all sulky was upset

donate give

as a side business and hobby for fun and to earn extra money

Alyce took me in to see him, and after an examination he declared my teeth in terrible shape. He said my gums were a wreck and he would have to deep-clean them. "Make an appointment," he said, "and I'll do the work for free." And he did.

Anyway, one day Dr. Gossett called John and said, "I have found a car. It's in Holland, Michigan."

As it happened, John was going to Holland that day on business, so he stopped by to look at the car. He took some pictures and brought them back to me—and, oh my gosh, the car was red!

I said, "I *want* that car. Whatever it takes, that's the car I want!"

Well, John could not **act on the matter** right away because he had another business trip scheduled, but when he came back, two days later, he called Dr. Gossett at once and said, "Okay, she wants that Dodge Neon."

Dr. Gossett said, "You waited too long. That car found a buyer."

I **pouted** for two days. Alyce called Dr. Gossett and said, "She's devastated. Can't you **dig up** another car for her? This is serious."

Dr. Gossett said, "Actually, I think I have just the one—it's a Mercedes-Benz."

Oh, Alyce and John came to me, all smiles! "Don't you fret anymore," they said. "Dr. Gossett has found another car for you."

....

act on the matter do anything
pouted was upset
dig up find

"What color is it?" That was all I wanted to know.

They couldn't answer that question. "It's a Mercedes," they informed me.

I didn't know the word "Mercedes." I thought they were naming a color. I said, "What's Mercedes?"

They said, "Never mind. Just go have a look at it. See what you think."

So the next time Dr. Gossett worked on my teeth, he took me to his house after the session. The car disappointed me: It was no Dodge Neon, I'll say that much. It looked small. I didn't mind the size, actually—I even liked a smaller car—but I didn't like the **looks of it**: the boxy style, that old-fashioned grill, and the color—it was a sort of dull gold. I felt all disappointed and sullen. The big red car appealed to my fantasies—it looked modern to me and, best of all, it was *red*! I love red.

Everyone was saying, "But, girl, this is a Mercedes, a famous brand. It will run for a long time without breaking down."

I said to myself, *Well, the red car is gone. I will have to settle for a Mercedes. It won't be so bad. At least it's a car.*

Later, when I told people I had a Mercedes-Benz, they always gasped. Other Afghans were agog to learn what model of car I was driving: They couldn't believe it. Gradually, I came to realize that I have something quite special here. It's pretty old, of course, but it runs very well. I found out later as well that it belonged to Dr. Gossett's wife. She bought herself a new car, and that's when she decided to give the old one to us.

Now that I have a car, I can go to the grocery store by

....

looks of it way it looked

myself. I can drive to Alyce's house. When the weather is nice, I drive to school, too, although if it's raining or snowing, I still take the bus: I don't want to **take any chances**.

In fact, I have gotten to know this whole area pretty well since I got a car. I can find my way to the place that sells *halal* meat. I can go to the houses of the other Afghans we have come to know. Everything I need is within fifteen minutes of my house, it turns out. I have not yet driven to downtown Chicago, but in my own area I'm not afraid to go anywhere.

....

take any chances risk wrecking the car

BEFORE YOU MOVE ON...

1. **Problem and Solution** Farah had difficulty driving because of her leg. How did she overcome this?

2. **Comparisons** Reread pages 259–260. How was Farah's life different after she got her driver's license?

LOOK AHEAD Read to page 273 to find out about a difficult decision Farah makes.

The Fashion Show

⌇⌇⌇

During our second summer in America, we moved to a new
apartment in a new town. At that point I **switched** schools,
too. I had started out in Lombard High. Now I'm going to
Wheaton North. The ESL department at my new high school
has an international club. Kids from other countries meet every
Wednesday after school to play games, talk, and have fun.
Ms. Ascadam, the teacher who sponsors this group, came from
Sudan when she was four or five years old. World Relief helped
her get to America. Now she's all grown up, she has finished
college, and she has a good job. It was she who organized this
multicultural club, and she still runs it.

I **had nothing to do with** the multicultural club when I
first came to Wheaton High School because I could not stay

....

switched changed

had nothing to do with did not join

at school **after hours**. I always had to rush home to study and take care of my mother's needs. Late last year, however, in the second semester, my life eased up somewhat and I decided to join the club. Right around that time Ms. Ascadam had decided that the international kids should throw a party at the end of the year and present a show. She told us each to bring food from our country to the party, and she encouraged us to think about participating in the show as well.

She announced that the first part of the show would be a dance performance by the kids from Mexico. The next part would be a fashion show. Kids from any country could be in the fashion show, and they would model clothes from their own culture, but no one had to do it.

I felt torn and confused. I could not take part in the dance, of course, but should I be in the fashion show? I really wanted to do it. I did have two beautiful Afghan outfits I could model. But I was also thinking, *My leg is damaged. What if I fall down?*

Finally, I said to myself, *Okay, next Wednesday I'll sit in on the practice session and see what it's like, and then I'll decide.*

That day the girl who always **denigrates me**, the one who said I would never learn to drive, came to the practice session, because she was planning to be in the fashion show. The moment she saw me sitting there, she could tell I was thinking of entering the show, too. She didn't ask if that's what I wanted, and she didn't **tell me to my face** that I could not do it, but she immediately called a few of the girls together to discuss what they would wear, and she **pointedly excluded me**. When

....

after hours after the school day ended
denigrates me puts me down; criticizes me
tell me to my face say directly to me
pointedly excluded me did not talk to me on purpose

I came over, she turned her back on me and pulled the ring of girls tighter to make sure that I would be left standing outside the circle, unable to join in.

At that moment I realized she did not want me in the show. The mere fact that I wanted to participate **outraged her**. Suddenly, she called out to the teacher. "Ms. Ascadam," she said, "when you model clothes at a fashion show, isn't this how you have to walk? Isn't this how models walk on a runway?"

Then she began to walk the way she thought a model should walk—with long strides, placing one foot in front of the other in a straight line that made her back end swing from side to side. "Is this the way you should walk?" she said. "If someone can't walk like this, should she be in the fashion show? She would just spoil the whole thing, wouldn't she?" And she kept walking back and forth, swinging from side to side.

It made me so angry, because I knew that she was really saying, *Farah can't do this. She has a problem with her legs. She shouldn't be in the fashion show.* She didn't say my name, but she was talking about me and only me, and everyone knew it.

That girl **broke my heart**. I felt as if somebody had punched me or slapped me. I felt as if someone had gotten into my throat and started pushing me and pressing me and choking me. I could not stay in that room. I turned and fled, my eyes stinging with tears. All the way home I cried. At home I threw myself on my bed and cried some more. I couldn't do my homework that day. I couldn't clean the house or cook or do anything. I just lay there, weeping and feeling

....

outraged her made her very angry
broke my heart made me very sad

sorry for myself—sorry about being **only half a woman**. I felt like everyone knew that I was not whole and that's what they thought about every time they looked at me. That girl had finally succeeded in **getting through my defenses** and poking me right where it hurt the most and where I would always hurt.

And what happened just then?

Alyce called.

"Hey," she said. "How are you, sweetie? Are you well?"

I started to bawl.

She said, "What is it? What are you crying about?"

I said, "Nothing, nothing. Never mind. Just nothing."

But she would not let it go. "No," she said, "you have to tell me."

So I said, "Okay, here's what happened." And I spilled the whole story.

Alyce said, "Now, don't **get all hung up on** what other people say. You just go ahead and do it. You tell your teacher you want to be in the fashion show."

But I just went on crying. "You don't understand. It's not *just* what 'other people say.' The terrible thing is, that girl is right! I *can't* be in a fashion show! It's true. How can someone like me be in a fashion show? With my limp? I can't walk like a model." That girl's cruelty wounded me, to be sure, but what really hurt was the truth she was telling. "Why are you trying to inspire me to do something I should never even try?" I ranted at Alyce.

It was one of those moments, you see. And Alyce just let me rage. But then she said, "No, that's not how the story goes

....

only half a woman an injured woman
getting through my defenses hurting me
get all hung up on be too worried about

around these parts. People aren't looking at you that way. Here, we **value** who you are as a person. You go right ahead and enter the fashion show fearlessly."

Well, I thought about it. I thought I should do it just to spite the girl who made those mean remarks and tried to keep me out of the show. I decided I had to do it, even if it meant falling down in the middle of the runway—because if I let that girl get away with talking about me as if I were half human, she would never stop. She would make me **her scapegoat** for the rest of my time at Wheaton North, and others would take up her view as well. I had to stand up for myself no matter what happened, because this was not just about a fashion show. It was about claiming my humanity. I had to do it.

I went to my teacher the next day and told her I wanted to enter the fashion show. She just looked at me for a moment, and then she rose out of her seat and hugged me. "Farah," she said, "this makes me so, so happy!"

After that I began to make my preparations. I had the clothes already, so I just put them on and started to practice walking. No, I started to practice *strutting* down a runway.

On the day of the fashion show my mother had a doctor's appointment, and Alyce took her there. The doctor was running a bit late. My mother got anxious. She wanted to see me up there modeling Afghan clothes, and she was afraid the doctor would make her miss the show. She urged Alyce to tell the doctor to hurry up. But of course a doctor isn't going to hurry up so that one of his patients can get to a fashion show on

---

value care
her scapegoat feel bad
strutting walking proudly

time. Alyce could do nothing. She and my mother just had to sit there and **bide their time**.

The show was **slated** to start at four o'clock. At a quarter to four my family had still not arrived. I stood backstage, peeking through a crack in the curtains and wringing my hands. Without my family—without Alyce and John and my mother—it just would not be the same.

Then I saw them. They arrived exactly at four! **Drenched with relief**, I hurried to the dressing room to get ready. I had time, because the dancing group was going on first. I had two dresses to wear, an orange one and a purple one. Backstage the makeup people put cosmetics on my face and curled my hair, so that I looked really different than usual. The teacher saw me and said, "Oh my gosh, you look so pretty!"

The dance performance ended, and the fashion show began. Each model was supposed to go out and walk around the stage in a certain pattern—a diamond-shaped pattern. We were each supposed to move to the front of the stage, then to one side, then to the back, and then to the other side. At each point of the diamond we were supposed to pause, face the audience, and **strike a pose**.

When my turn came, I went strutting out. I threw my shoulders back and held my head up high so that my neck stretched long. I didn't fall, and I didn't shake. I didn't even feel nervous. When I finished my pattern, I went backstage, changed into my other dress, went back out, and did the whole thing again.

....

bide their time wait

slated scheduled, planned

Drenched with relief Happy and feeling better

strike a pose stand proudly

Alyce told me later that no one could **tell about my legs**. I moved **in time to** the music, showed the clothes off well, and smiled—I did just fine! My mother **beamed**. She didn't say much at the time, but later on, at home, she told me she felt proud of me. Imagine that! Proud that her daughter stood up before an audience of strangers and modeled our beautiful Afghan clothes: She, too, has come a long way since we arrived in America.

After the show the party began. We had all brought special foods from our various cultures. My mother had cooked a fancy Afghan rice dish. We all ate and chatted and felt happy. That night, even though it wasn't literally true, I felt that I was wearing high-heeled shoes at last.

....

tell about my legs see that my legs were injured
in time to with
beamed smiled a lot

LOOKING BACK,
LOOKING AHEAD

❧

My life remains a struggle in many ways, but things are better now. Things are so much better. Some of the improvements are just details, but details add up. In the end, **details make a life**.

Take our apartment, for example. When we first came to America, we lived on the **ground** floor of a building in Glendale Heights. We were too close to the street. Our windows **looked right out onto** a parking lot. We could hear people fighting out there, and the noise of traffic disturbed us at all hours. Sometimes at night the cars sounded like they were going to drive right through our walls and into our bedroom.

Then we moved to Carol Stream, which is about ten minutes from Glendale Heights by car. We moved into an apartment on the second floor of a three-story building, and

....

details make a life life is made up of small events
ground lowest, bottom
looked right out onto had a view of

we like it better. My mother feels a bit safer here, and for her, believe me, every little bit of "safer" **counts**.

My mother is **sort of blank** now and can't remember much, which is hard for both of us, but she's better than she used to be. When we first came to America, I worried that they would take her to the hospital and keep her there. I thought I would lose her, and I wondered what I would do here all alone.

Back then she could never sleep at night. She only slept a little in the daytime. At night she paced back and forth, talking to herself, muttering and crying. She kept me awake much of the time, and if I did manage to fall asleep, she woke me up with the curses and **imprecations** she uttered in the dark. Sometimes she came into my room in the middle of the night to inquire softly, "Can I sleep in here?"

And I always said, "Yes, fine. You can sleep in here, but *sleep*, please! So I can sleep, too." Because I needed my rest. I couldn't afford to stay awake with her dusk to dawn, night after night.

And even if she didn't come into my room, and even if she did fall asleep, she kept me awake by talking and even crying out in her sleep.

In the daytime, however, she was quiet. We had no mother-daughter conversations, like her saying, *Oh, you should wear this dress* or *This is a nice color for you* or *Let down your hair; it looks nice that way.* Never. But if I plucked my eyebrows because I wanted to look pretty, then she spoke to me. "Stop plucking your eyebrows," she said. "Let them grow back!"

If I came home with something from the store, like a new

....

counts is important

sort of blank confused

imprecations evil sayings

top, she spoke to me then, too. "Why did you buy that? All day long you're shopping and buying things—stop shopping! Don't buy anything!"

Mostly, however, she said nothing. And even now, when I come home from school, I usually find her just sitting quietly in her room or watching a cooking show on TV. She never asks what I am thinking or how I am feeling. She's afraid, I think, to say anything that might **arouse my anxieties**. I certainly am afraid to say anything that might stir up hers.

But my mother is a good mother. She's quiet now because she has lost her whole family except me, her home, her way of life—everything. For me, it's easier to adjust. I'm young. But my mother had **a set and sheltered** way of life for so many years, and then she lost everything. That's why she's quiet.

I remember when I was little, how she combed and braided my hair, how she bought me frilly dresses, how she put kohl on my eyelids to blacken them and make my eyes look beautiful. She took me places. In Afghanistan she was **a celebrated hostess**: She threw parties, entertained guests lavishly, and kept a clean house—well, she still keeps a clean house. She's a good mother, but she's different now. She's quiet.

And I don't like the differences in her, but she's getting better. She sees a psychiatrist, and he gives her medications that help her sleep. She had no patience when we were in Pakistan and even less when we first came here, but she is growing more patient all the time. I think she is still in shock somehow. Deep in her mind, she's resting and waiting for **the dust to settle**,

....

arouse my anxieties make me worried
a set and sheltered an organized and quiet
a celebrated hostess known for her parties
the dust to settle her life to feel ordinary again

and that's what she needs, because she was so frightened for such a long time.

She's getting better. When we first came to America, she didn't trust me. She worried every time I went out. She thought I was out looking for a boyfriend. She didn't trust me with Alyce, either. When I came back from **an outing** with the Litzes, she would always interrogate me suspiciously. "Where did you go? What did you do? Who did you see?" But she has come to trust Alyce and John, as well as me. Lately, she doesn't worry when I go out with them, no matter where we go or how long I stay out.

My mother now has a bit of a social life of her own. She has gotten to know some other Afghan women in the neighborhood. On warm days they all walk to the park together with their thermoses. They sit on the grass and chat and have tea.

On weekends other Afghan families drop by, or we go to their houses to visit. Sometimes we all go to the park and cook **kebabs** of every kind. In late March, which is Afghan New Year's, we get together to celebrate with a barbecue. On the first night of the Eid festival, the holiest holiday in Islam, the Afghans have a big party in downtown Chicago.

In the last couple of months my mother has even started going to school. She is going to an English-language course three times a week. Yes, my mother is definitely beginning to perk up a bit and come alive again. She is like a plant that is finally getting some water.

I like seeing such changes in my mother. Now, finally, she

....

an outing a trip; an activity
kebabs meat and vegetables on a stick

tells me she's glad I brought her to America. That makes me so happy. I feel that I have brought her to safety. I see her sitting quietly, breathing easily, looking calm, and I say to myself, *I did do one thing right in my life: I saved my mother.*

I don't know what **the future holds for me**. With God's grace, I plan to go to college, but I don't know what I'll study yet. It depends on what talents I have and how smart I am. I have to try different things and see. I might like to work with computers, or I might like to go into business. I would certainly like to be a doctor, but you have to be pretty smart for that—I don't know if I could do it. Maybe I could design prostheses. A good prosthesis means so much to someone who has lost a limb. Mine gave me a new life. I would like to give someone a new life.

But there are many different ways to renew somebody's life, so I have to explore. I just know I want to help people who have a disability to feel that they are still people, that they still have a life, and that they should keep going.

I hope to see Afghanistan again one day. When I'm done with college and have a career, I would like to go there for a visit and see what I can do to help. They need doctors and medical stuff, of course, and so many people over there need prostheses. Maybe I could help in those areas.

But if I don't do that, I at least want to talk to the parents in Afghanistan. I want to tell them to send their children to school. And that's not all. They need to get their kids excited about school. Celebrate when they do well, notice them, reward

....

the future holds for me life will be like in the future

testify to tell them from experience

them. I can **testify to** how hard it is to go into ninth grade if you have missed grades two through eight. I don't want other Afghan children to go through something like that. I want to warn Afghan parents: If you make your children go to work in a grocery store or a mechanic's shop or a carpet-weaving factory or something, you will get some money now, but someday your children will regret not having gone to school, and on that day they will blame you.

When I first came to America, I wanted to forget my past. I wanted to take a big eraser and rub out every memory I had. I wanted to become totally American **through and through** as quickly as I could.

But time passed, and I began to think about it. I realized that it's good to remember my own customs and traditions. It's good to hold on to my own religion and faith. It's not good to forget where I have come from and who I have been. It's all a part of who I really am.

Now I don't want to erase, or forget, or destroy any part of myself. I want to love myself and keep **adding to** who I am. Today I feel that I am both Afghan and American. And today is not necessarily **where it ends**.

···

testify to tell them from experience
through and through as completely and
adding to learning
where it ends the end of my story

BEFORE YOU MOVE ON...

1. **Paraphrase** Farah writes that joining the fashion show was about "claiming my humanity." What does she mean by this?

2. **Simile** Reread page 271. How is Farah's mother "like a plant that is finally getting some water"?